Martin Luth  *...ologians*

"Rufus Burrow Jr. has done it again—he has provided us with another creative, compelling, and clear portrait of the greatest civil rights leader in world history. Martin Luther King Jr. appears in this rich book as a serious theologian, an inspirational activist, and yet a man who did not escape the prejudices of his time. Students, activists, and Christians everywhere would do well to grab this invaluable book, settle in an armchair for the evening, and expect to be held spellbound by King's prophetic witness to the love and justice of Jesus."

—Michael G. Long, Associate Professor of Religious Studies and Peace and Conflict Studies at Elizabethtown College and the author of *Against Us, but for Us: Martin Luther King, Jr. and the State*

"*Martin Luther King Jr. for Armchair Theologians* is a usable and reader-friendly text, a first-rate choice for the classroom or for small group study. Students, both young and old, will profit from this compact theo-biography that features reflective illustrations by Ron Hill and meticulous research by Rufus Burrow Jr."

—Linda Sue Hewitt, Pastor, Bourbon First United Church of Christ, Bourbon, Indiana

Also Available in the Armchair Series

Aquinas for Armchair Theologians by Timothy M. Renick
Augustine for Armchair Theologians by Stephen A. Cooper
Barth for Armchair Theologians by John R. Franke
Bonhoeffer for Armchair Theologians by Stephen R. Haynes and Lori Brandt Hale
Calvin for Armchair Theologians by Christopher Elwood
Heretics for Armchair Theologians by Justo L. González and Catherine Gusalus González
Jonathan Edwards for Armchair Theologians by James P. Byrd
Luther for Armchair Theologians by Steven Paulson
The Reformation for Armchair Theologians by Glenn S. Sunshine
Wesley for Armchair Theologians by William J. Abraham

Martin Luther King Jr. for Armchair Theologians

RUFUS BURROW JR.

ILLUSTRATIONS BY RON HILL

WESTMINSTER
JOHN KNOX PRESS
LOUISVILLE • KENTUCKY

Book design by Sharon Adams
Cover design by Jennifer K. Cox
Cover illustration by Ron Hill

First edition
Published by Westminster John Knox Press
Louisville, Kentucky

This book is printed on acid-free paper that meets the American National Standards Institute Z39.48 standard. ♾

PRINTED IN THE UNITED STATES OF AMERICA

11 12 13 14 15 16 17 18 — 10 9 8 7 6 5 4 3 2

Library of Congress Cataloging-in-Publication Data

Burrow, Rufus.
    Martin Luther King Jr. for armchair theologians / Rufus Burrow Jr.
— 1st ed.
        p. cm.
    Includes bibliographical references and index.
    ISBN 978-0-664-23284-9 (alk. paper)
    1. King, Martin Luther, Jr., 1929–1968. 2. King, Martin Luther, Jr., 1929–1968—Philosophy. 3. King, Martin Luther, Jr., 1929–1968—Ethics. 4. Nonviolence. 5. Civil disobedience. 6. United States—Race relations—History—20th century. 7. African Americans—Civil rights—History—20th century. 8. African Americans—Biography. 9. Civil rights workers—United States—Biography. 10. Baptists—United States—Biography.
    I. Title.

E185.97.K5B799 2009
323.092—dc22
[B]

                                                    2008039365

To the memory of Frederick Douglas Smith (1936–2007), educator, mentor, friend, and humanitarian who cared about the children from the projects on the west side of Pontiac, Michigan, and who, through his witness, commitment, and example showed us the way.

Contents

Acknowledgments   vii

Preface   ix

1. Our Racist History   1

2. Ideas from Home   23

3. Ideas from the Academy   43

4. Montgomery   61

5. Christian Love and Gandhian Nonviolence   79

6. The Power and Persuasion of Youth   97

7. Against Racism, Economic Exploitation, and War   123

8. Women, Capital Punishment, and Homosexuality   141

9. The Legacy of Martin Luther King Jr.   161

Notes   179

Select Bibliography   189

Index   191

Acknowledgments

I had the good fortune to have three superb teachers and scholars read multiple drafts of this manuscript. Professors Mary Alice Mulligan (a homiletician and Christian ethicist forging new and exciting paths) of Christian Theological Seminary (Indianapolis) and Lewis V. Baldwin (renowned King scholar) of Vanderbilt University (Nashville) each read the manuscript for factual accuracy and coherency. In addition, each offered helpful advice regarding the readability of the manuscript for the college and seminary student. Reverend Linda Sue Hewitt (a minister of the Christian Church (Disciples of Christ) and the United Church of Christ and a career teacher in the Rochester, Indiana, public school system) made a number of helpful suggestions for how the manuscript could be made more readable and accessible to the high school student. There are no adequate words to express my deep gratitude to these excellent teachers.

Many thanks to Donald McKim who, at a time when I felt I simply could not accept one more thing on my plate, invited me to write this book for the Westminster John Knox series on Armchair Theologians. He was so generous and cool in his approach and his willingness to give me as much time as I needed to think over his invitation that I found it impossible to say no. Don made the writing of this manuscript both enjoyable and tremendously challenging.

It was a joy working with Ron Hill, illustrator for the

Acknowledgments

series. A teacher of inner-city youth at a high school in Ohio, Ron is a person of deep sensitivity and awareness. Many of his illustrations make the ideas in the book live in ways they otherwise would not. Through his illustrations readers will easily see that Ron Hill got the point of each individual chapter and the book as a whole.

PREFACE

Martin Luther King Jr. was a man of serious philosophical, theological, and ethical ideas who was intentional about living and applying these in his efforts to bring about the beloved community—that is, the world as God would have it. Ideas always influenced his Christian social activism, even as the latter helped to inform and refine those ideas for further application to the struggle for civil and human rights. It is therefore erroneous to say, as many have, that King was primarily a social activist rather than a thinker. The truth is that he was the quintessential man of ideas *and* of social activism. Indeed, in an interview with Hugh Downs on April 18, 1966, King said that he was a theist and consequently believed firmly in the reality and existence of God, even though he did not believe it possible to prove it through philosophical argument. This was a clear reminder of his love for ideas and intellectual argument. Martin Luther King never tried to separate ideas (from the academy) from activism (in the streets). Instead, he always brought his best thinking to bear on noncooperation campaigns, permitting his ideas and thinking to be informed and transformed by his practice, and refining his practice with his well-thought-out ideas.

Although King earned the PhD degree in systematic theology, it became increasingly clear to him that his deepest commitment was to practicing theological social ethics, which did not mean that he ever lost the desire to teach and to write books on theology. Rather, the deeper calling was to apply all that he had learned to the attainment of a world house based on God's expectation that love and justice be done throughout the world. Practically, therefore, he was a theological social ethicist with a doctorate in systematic theology.

This book is aimed at a popular audience, but it is a valuable resource for high school seniors as well as college and graduate students who are seeking a basic introduction to the theological and ethical ideas and practice of Martin Luther King. The goal is to arouse interest in pursuing more serious study on King and his legacy for the twenty-first century and beyond. It is not expected that readers will know much about the historical context that led King into local, national, and international leadership. Consequently, the first chapter will provide a general historical overview of black-white race relations in the United States up to the time that King was selected as the leader of the Montgomery bus boycott in December 1955.[1]

Chapters 2 and 3 focus on homegrown and formal intellectual ideas, respectively, that influenced who King came to be as person, thinker, minister, and social activist. From here the discussion turns in chapter 4 to contributions of some of the forerunners to King's involvement and leadership in the bus boycott. These include but are not limited to Vernon Johns, Mary Fair Burks, JoAnn Robinson, Claudette Colvin, and Rosa Parks. Particular attention is given to black women of Montgomery and their trailblazing role.

King's evolution toward Gandhian nonviolence after the Montgomery bus boycott had been underway for two months is the subject of chapter 5. King originally focused on the ethics of the Sermon on the Mount, until he was advised on Gandhian principles and techniques. Considerable attention is given to the basic elements of King's doctrine of nonviolent resistance to evil. This discussion leads easily to the next chapter, which focuses on King's love and respect for youth and their role in the struggle from Montgomery to Memphis. The emphasis is on the power and contributions of young people from elementary school through college. Just as young people started the direct action sit-in movement in 1960, and participated in the freedom rides in 1961, this chapter shows how deep was their involvement and contributions in action sites such as Montgomery, Birmingham, the Mississippi Delta, and Selma.

The next two chapters discuss King's stance on racism, economic exploitation and poverty, war and peace, gender issues, capital punishment, and homosexuality. One finds very little written on the latter two subjects in King studies. Although King said little about these, the very nature of his theological social ethic requires consideration of them.

Much of the discussion in chapter 9 is in the form of a prophetic challenge. King intentionally sought to apply the basic principles of his theology and faith to making the world a gentler, more just and humane place, particularly for those living in and at the margins. Although he was concerned about the well-being of people in general, we will see that there are specific aspects of his legacy that may be appropriated most especially by Afrikan Americans.[2]

CHAPTER ONE

Our Racist History

The name "Martin Luther King Jr." and the term "civil rights movement" have often been used interchangeably, as if to imply that King was "the movement," or that he was its sole leader. Although neither of these was true, he was indeed a major symbol and leader of the movement. Still, almost from its inception there were a host of women and men who provided leadership in various areas of the movement. It is important to keep this in mind, although our focus here is on King.

Most twenty-first-century students from high school to

graduate school know little about Martin Luther King Jr. and the civil and human rights movements. Throughout their formal education they receive little exposure to race relations and King. In light of this failure of the educational system, it is reasonable to assume that many who read this book do not know much about the historical setting that led to the mass bus boycott in Montgomery that propelled a young, well-trained black clergyman into local, national, and international leadership. Martin Luther King did not seek out such a role. Rather, a confluence of events in Montgomery, Alabama, seems to have sought him out. He said often that he was tracked down by "the spirit of the times."

This chapter provides a cursory overview of black-white relations from the time Afrikans were stolen primarily from West Afrikan countries and forced into dehumanizing enslavement in Europe and the Americas more than six hundred years ago. From the beginning the Europeans assumed an attitude of racial superiority and tried to paint the Afrikans as savages who needed whites to civilize them.

Most young people of any race today know little about this history and how racism and white privilege became institutionalized through official documents such as the Declaration of Independence and the Constitution of the United States. In addition, during enslavement the judicial system and all levels of government forbade blacks to marry, learn to read, or own property. Black skin was perceived as a liability. What all whites have shared in common during and subsequent to the enslavement period, Andrew Hacker observes, is their white skin. This means that in the crunch all white people can boast, "At least I am not black." One's white skin ensures that he or she "will not be regarded as *black*, a security that is worth so much that no one who has it has ever given it away," says Hacker. Therefore, "to be black is to be consigned to the margins of

American life. It is because of this that no white American . . . would change places with even the most successful black American."[1] This is a very significant claim, for it means that white skin is a symbol of privilege to be respected in this society in ways that black skin never has been. As used in this book, "white privilege" entails unearned benefits, advantages, and privileges inherited by generations of white people from the time of enslavement. White privilege also entails a sense of being entitled to these benefits, which may be material, symbolic, psychological, or a combination of these.

Sociologist Joe Feagin points out that few whites have a sense of "the reality of this whole society being founded on, and firmly grounded in, oppression targeting African

3

Americans (and other Americans of color) now for several centuries."[2] In fact, race oppression is not an accident of United States history, "but was created intentionally by powerful white Americans" beginning in the seventeenth century.[3] Powerful white Americans felt justified in creating this state of affairs, and many work hard to sustain and enhance it today. Race oppression and white privilege are embedded in the very foundation of this nation. After all, fifty-five white men (40 percent of whom were enslavers) met in Philadelphia in 1787 to create the Constitution. No Afrikans, other people of color, or women of any race were present. American society and the Constitution on which it is based were from the beginning "structured in terms of white gains and white group interests. Once this system was put into place . . . white privileges soon came to be sensed as usual and natural."[4]

If one does not have a sense of the history of systemic racism and white privilege and how these developed in this country, it will be virtually impossible to appreciate Martin Luther King's struggle for civil and human rights nationally and internationally, and why forty years after King's assassination Afrikan Americans still complain about being victimized by racism, by its many tragic manifestations and consequences. In these early years of the twenty-first century many young white people have little sense of why there is tension between themselves and their Afrikan American peers. In part this is due to their not having lived through periods of sustained blatant racism as King did when he was growing up in the 1930s and 1940s. Another contributing factor is the failure of the educational system—at every level—to teach students this history. Consequently, it is important to set the historical stage for the ensuing discussion on Martin Luther King as a man of faith, ideas, and social activism.

4

The Slavery Question

The various peoples of Afrika had long and distinguished histories and cultures prior to being forced into enslavement in the so-called New World in the fifteenth century. How and why did the Afrikans come to be in this part of the world, and what affect did this have on their culture and fundamental beliefs? How were they treated by the whites who enslaved them?

The practice of enslaving human beings likely existed in the earliest days of history on all continents. The elements of cruelty and oppression undoubtedly existed wherever enslavement occurred. However, scholars maintain that the Europeans introduced new elements into the enslavement

5

practice. These included: (1) the sheer inhumanity of the way they practiced the enslavement of Afrikans; (2) the fact that the West Afrikans were traded and sold like any other commodity at the market; and (3) the perpetual and automatic enslavement of Afrikans' offspring.

Some scholars argue that persons captured during tribal wars in old Afrika were frequently enslaved, but these persons retained most of their human rights and were often treated more like domestic servants and family members than like people forced into enslavement. It is also of interest to note that generally Afrikan rulers who participated in the European enslavement trade only rarely sold people from their own society, and these were usually from the ranks of criminals and outcasts. In addition, the enslaved were not removed from the land in which they were born, reared, and lived their lives before captivity. In this regard, being enslaved and the enslavement trade were not precisely the same thing. We therefore need to distinguish between enslavement practiced during precolonial times or the period of old Afrika, and the enslavement trade on the western coast of Afrika that was introduced by the Europeans.

The type of enslavement practiced on the Afrikan continent and that practiced by the Europeans were to a large extent qualitatively different from each other. The Afrikans captured and enslaved during tribal wars remained on the continent and thus in relatively familiar surroundings. In addition, they were generally treated like human beings. But the Europeans not only forcibly removed them from the continent, packing them into steamy, putrid holds of large ships for the excruciatingly long, dehumanizing voyage across the Atlantic Ocean (the Middle Passage), but upon being sold the Afrikans, especially those whose destination was the American colonies, were frequently subjected to unspeakable brutalities. It is not far-fetched to argue, as Kevin Shillington does, that, "the greatest evil of the transatlantic trade in people was the extent of human suffering involved, and the callous disregard for human life and dignity displayed by those who dealt in slaves."[5] To make things worse, Afrikans sold in the Atlantic trade were not only in completely unfamiliar surroundings, but the color of their skin made it virtually impossible for them to blend in with the surrounding population even if they succeeded in escaping their enslavers. In addition, they could not possibly get back to the Afrikan continent.

The Afrikans resisted at virtually every stage of their capture by the Europeans. Recognizing their own sense of humanity and dignity, they did not willingly go into enslavement. Martin Luther King held that they resisted as best they could, but because they had no organized military, and no desire to steal the land of other people and perpetuate racism

all over the world, "they were conquered, and taken, and chained to ships like beasts."[6] But at every point, King argued, the Afrikans resisted their captivity, both during the journey across the Atlantic and in the colonies.

Whites presented the Afrikans as savages and then tried to justify enslaving them as a means of rescuing them from savagery. From the beginning to the end of the enslavement trade (approximately three hundred years), the Afrikan continent was depopulated by an estimated thirty to forty million people, mostly younger, stronger persons. This was the greatest forced redistribution of a people in history. The effect on the Afrikan continent and Afrikans in diaspora was devastating, and the consequences are still being felt.

By 1640—barely twenty years after the arrival of the first Afrikans in the colony of Virginia—the indentured status of the Afrikans was already showing signs of changing to the more permanent state of enslavement. One sign of this was the case of Afrikan indentured servant John Punch who, along with two white servants, escaped to Maryland. When they were captured and returned to Virginia, all three received thirty lashes. In addition, the two white servants were ordered to serve out their indenture plus one year, and afterward "to serve the colony for three whole years apiece." The major difference in the sentence of John Punch was that he was ordered to "serve his said master or his assigns for the time of his natural life here or elsewhere."[7]

In effect, Punch, unlike the two white servants, was condemned to permanent enslavement. One cannot help but see the racial implications in this, despite the fact that Virginia was slower than some other colonies in coming to see the advantage of the perpetual enslavement of the Afrikans. White indentured servants often tried to sue for one reason or another. In addition, many of the white men England sent for indentured servitude were of the criminal and

lower classes. Furthermore, when white indentured servants would run away it was easy for them to blend in with the population. Neither the Indians nor the Afrikans were so fortunate. Between 1660 and 1662, statutes in Virginia recognized the existence of enslavement and supported its continued development.

In his *Notes on the State of Virginia* (1787) Thomas Jefferson spoke for many whites when he responded negatively to the question of whether Afrikans should be incorporated into the state of Virginia as citizens. In the process of responding to this query, Jefferson also gave his own views on the moral, spiritual, and intellectual capacity of the Afrikans. The reason for not incorporating them into the state was quite simple, according to Jefferson: "Deep rooted prejudices entertained by the whites; ten thousand recollections, by the blacks, of the injuries they have sustained; new provocations; the real distinctions which nature has made; and many other circumstances, will divide us into parties, and produce convulsions which will probably never

9

end but in the extermination of the one or the other race."
Jefferson believed the Afrikans were inherently "inferior to
the whites in the endowments of body, mind, and imagina-
tion."[8] Statements such as this led King to say that "the
social obstetricians who presided at the birth of racist views
in our country were from the aristocracy," and not solely
the poor, uneducated whites.[9]

According to Jefferson, the Afrikans knew nothing of
sentimental love, for "love seems with them to be more an
eager desire, than a tender delicate mixture of sentiment
and sensation." In addition, Jefferson said he had never
known an instance in which "a black had uttered a thought
above the level of plain narration," nor had he seen evidence of their ability to be artists or sculptors, although
they seemed more musically inclined than whites.[10] Furthermore, Jefferson argued that there was no poetry
among the Afrikans. At this point he disparaged the poetic
works of Phyllis Wheatley, concluding that any progress
toward civilization made by the Afrikans was due to their
association with whites.

Clearly, neither Jefferson, Washington, nor any of the
other Founding Fathers had a clear sense of the full
humanity and dignity of blacks. According to King, "not
one of these men had a strong unequivocal belief in the
equality of the black man."[11] While applauding the words
"all men are created equal," King concluded that this
meant for Jefferson what it meant for most whites—"all
white men are created equal."[12]

The Declaration of Independence
and the Constitution

The Declaration of Independence (1776) declared self-
evident the truth that "all men are created equal, that they

are endowed by their Creator with certain unalienable rights, that among these are life, liberty, and the pursuit of happiness." When the time came to draft the Constitution a dispute arose in the Congress between Southerners and Northerners over how or whether to count enslaved Afrikans in determining the number of representatives each state could send to Congress. Since most of the enslaved were in the South, it was advantageous to southern representatives to have them counted when determining the number of representatives. However, the Southerners did not want the enslaved Afrikans counted when determining taxes to be paid. Northern representatives saw that it would be to their advantage were it the other way around. The matter was settled by introducing the controversial *three-fifths compromise* clause. In article 1, section 2, paragraph 3 of the United States Constitution we find that the number of representatives "shall be determined by adding to the whole number of free persons, including those bound to service for a term of years, and excluding Indians not taxed, three fifths of all other persons."[13] "All other persons" were the enslaved

Afrikans, although it is interesting to note that since they were generally considered not to be full-fledged human beings, they were referred to in the document as "persons." Unquestionably, the drafters of the Constitution meant something qualitatively different by "person" where the Afrikans were concerned. By no means did they intend to grant constitutional rights to blacks.

Dred and Harriet Scott and the Supreme Court

The idea that the Afrikans were not fully human was institutionalized in this country long before the writing of the Constitution and was given further legitimacy by rulings of the Supreme Court, not least the ruling in *Dred Scott v. Sanford* (1857). Scott and his wife Harriet were enslaved Afrikans who "belonged" to an army surgeon named John Emerson. When Emerson was transferred from the enslavement state of Missouri to the free state of Illinois, he took the Scotts with him as his servants. When he moved to the free Wisconsin Territory he again took the Scotts with him. When Emerson died, some abolitionists helped the Scotts sue for their freedom. The suit was based on the idea that the Scotts had lived in a free state and in a free territory. Their lawyer argued that this made them free persons. The case went to the Supreme Court. The question before the Court was whether or not the opening words of the preamble to the Constitution, "We the people," included persons of Afrikan descent.

Chief Justice Roger B. Taney read the majority opinion, which made clear that persons of Afrikan descent were not citizens of the colonies when the Declaration and Constitution were written. Therefore they could not bring suit against whites in the courts. In addition, the Court said that even if the Scotts did have the right to sue, the fact that they lived in Illinois and the Wisconsin Territory did not make them free. After all, an enslaved Afrikan was thought to be the "property" of his owner, and the Constitution protected a person's property, even when it did not provide protection for specific groups of persons. As a property owner, then, one could take his property anywhere in the United States, but this would not in any way alter the status of said property. Once enslaved, always enslaved! According to Taney, the Afrikans were granted no rights either in the Declaration or the Constitution, and they had no rights that whites were bound to respect.

In its 7-2 ruling, the highest court of the land had declared that the famous statement on basic human rights in the Declaration of Independence did not include the Afrikans in the colonies, for they were considered by the "civilized portion of the white race" to be so far inferior to whites that their only value was in being enslaved to whites. The Afrikans were thought to be subhuman in comparison to whites. Essentially, then, racism was embedded in the basic human rights documents of the United States from the outset.

Reconstruction

Abraham Lincoln's Emancipation Proclamation in 1863 ostensibly liberated the Afrikans from enslavement. However, they were given nothing of substance to help them make the transition from enslavement to a life of freedom. King observed that with the signing of the Emancipation Proclamation "the nation didn't give the Negro one penny, or any land to make the freedom meaningful."[14] It was at best an abstract freedom.

After the Civil War, the Reconstruction era (1865–1877) was initiated by Congress to aid the transition to freedom. Although this turned out to be a short-lived experiment, blacks throughout the South made tremendous strides in the political process. For these few years, they were able to vote, run for and gain election to office, and have some degree of influence in the political process. This was aided by the passing of three civil rights amendments during the Reconstruction period: the thirteenth, passed in 1865, abolished enslavement; the fourteenth, passed in 1868, guaranteed equal protection under the law; and the fifteenth, passed in 1870, outlawed voting restrictions based on race or "previous condition of servitude." These amendments have been referred to as "a second Bill of Rights" for Afrikan Americans, although we will see that the federal government and the Supreme Court offered no leadership in enforcing the fourteenth and fifteenth amendments up to and during the Montgomery bus boycott in the mid-1950s.

Blacks served as elected officials at the city, state, and national levels during Reconstruction. The first blacks served in the U.S. Congress during this period. Twenty blacks served in the House of Representatives. Hiram Revels served one year in the Senate, and Blanche K. Bruce (both representing Mississippi) served a full term. It speaks

volumes that Bruce was the only Afrikan American to serve a full term in the Senate for almost a hundred years, until the election of Edward Brooke from Massachusetts in 1966, then Carol Moseley Braun of Illinois (the first black woman) in 1992, and Barack Obama of Illinois in 2004. Mr. Obama was sworn in as the 44th president of the United States on January 20, 2009.

Unfortunately, the Reconstruction period also saw the rise of the Ku Klux Klan, a white supremacist group founded in 1866 by Confederate veterans to terrorize blacks and their white allies. During this period the Klan worked mainly to keep blacks from voting. In addition, it also helped to restore power to conservative Democrats in the South.

The Compromise of 1877

The election of Rutherford B. Hayes to the presidency in 1877 was based on a two-pronged compromise: (1) that he would withdraw the federal troops from the South and pursue a policy of conciliation toward that region, and (2) that Congress would provide a federal subsidy to Northern and Southern businessmen to build the Texas and Pacific Railroad as well as make other improvements in the South. Hayes also promised both to get pledges from white Southern leaders to protect the civil rights of blacks and to use the authority of his office to ensure such protection. However, Hayes placed adherence to peace, order, and harmony above that of compliance with the civil rights amendments.

Although Hayes tried to make good his promise to ensure the protection of the rights of blacks, he naively trusted the white Southerners to keep their part of the bargain. Their aim was to return to "states' rights" or "home rule." Historian Rayford Logan depicts Hayes as "the principal presidential architect of the consolidation of white supremacy in the South, during the post-Reconstruction period."[15] By naively trusting white Southerners and withdrawing the troops, Hayes gave the South a clear path to decide how it wanted to relate to blacks during the post-Reconstruction period. Blacks and democracy were the sacrificial lambs in the Great Compromise. The South once again had the authority—without fear of federal intervention and reprisal—to decide how it would handle the matter of race, which it did up to and beyond the Montgomery bus boycott.

Separate but Equal

In 1890, Louisiana passed a law providing for separate accommodations for whites and blacks in public transportation. Then in 1892, Homer Plessy, who was one-eighth black and seven-eighths white, was arrested after refusing to leave a "whites only" train. Plessy and his supporters sought to test the constitutionality of the Separate Car Law on the basis that it contradicted the thirteenth and fourteenth amendments. The case went to the Supreme Court. In 1896, the Court ruled in favor of the Louisiana law in an 8-1 vote, thus establishing the constitutionality of the "separate but equal" doctrine that became the law of the land for fifty years.

The ruling in *Plessy v. Ferguson* essentially nullified the civil rights amendments of the Reconstruction era and became the foundation for the system of segregation and all that it stood for. Justice John Marshall Harlan, himself a former enslaver from Kentucky, wrote a blistering dissent in which he criticized his colleagues for retreating from the principle of racial equality, believing as he did that the law is colorblind when it comes to the civil rights of its citizens. Harlan concluded, "The destinies of the two races in this country are indissolubly linked together, and the interests of both require that the common government of all shall not permit the seeds of race hate to be planted under the sanction of law." Moreover, and quite prophetically, Harlan said that "the judgment of this day rendered will, in time, prove to be quite as pernicious as the decision made by this tribunal in the Dred Scott Case." Harlan was anticipating the reversal of the decision in *Plessy*.

In 1915, William J. Simmons expanded the Ku Klux Klan into a national organization. Its purpose was to frighten and intimidate blacks and their white allies. In

17

addition, the Klan hated Jews, immigrants, and Catholics. By the 1920s, the Klan was known for its terrorist activities against these groups, but its membership declined significantly when a number of its top leaders were successfully prosecuted and convicted of serious crimes, and when members were not able to pay dues during the Depression years of the early 1930s. Then, in the early 1950s, when Martin Luther King began his ministry in Montgomery, Alabama, a revived Klan terrorized and murdered some civil rights workers and black voters.

The 1950s

In the mid-1930s the legal defense team for the National Association for the Advancement of Colored People (NAACP) began challenging the "separate but equal" decision in *Plessy v. Ferguson* by challenging in state and federal courts the Jim Crow laws that legalized racial segregation in public facilities and in schools. In *Brown v. Board of Education* in 1954 the Court, under Chief Justice Earl Warren, unanimously ruled against "separate but equal." In a separate ruling one year later, referred to by some as *Brown II*, the Court instructed the states to begin implementing *Brown* "with all deliberate speed." Intended or not, this gave rebellious states just the opening they needed to construct schemes to delay desegregating public schools. Consequently, by 1964 only 1 percent of black children in the South attended integrated schools.

In August 1955, only a few months after the Court's "all deliberate speed" ruling, fourteen-year-old Emmett Till of Chicago was visiting an uncle in Money, Mississippi, when he allegedly touched and whistled at a white woman in a store. Till, a child, was kidnapped from his uncle's home and made the victim of one of the most brutal murders in the annals of civil rights history. He was shot in the head and his face so disfigured by the murderers that he was unrecognizable. When his body was returned home to Chicago, Till's mother, Mamie Bradley, rejected the advice that she have a closed-casket funeral. She opted to have it open because she wanted the whole world to see what racist whites had done to her son. Till's (self-confessed) murderers went to trial but were not convicted by the all-white jury.[16]

Martin Luther King had been pastor of Dexter Avenue Baptist Church in Montgomery for only one year before the brutal murder of Till. Deeply affected by this tragedy, he said in a number of sermons that too often those who

murder black children and throw their bodies into rivers (as happened with Till) attend church every Sunday. King was certain that they worshiped God aesthetically and emotionally but not morally. He was convinced that such people knew nothing of ethical Christianity.

Four months after the brutal murder of Emmett Till, Rosa Parks was arrested for violating the segregation ordinance in Montgomery, Alabama. This was the event that catapulted the civil rights movement and Martin Luther King into the national spotlight. But before these events, King's leadership abilities were being shaped. It is to King's background and upbringing, the foundations of his intellectual development and his social activism, that we now turn.

CHAPTER TWO

Ideas from Home

Michael King Jr. was born on January 15, 1929, in Atlanta, Georgia. His sister, Willie Christine, was born in 1927 and his brother, Alfred Daniel (A. D.), in 1930. In contrast to millions of other black babies across the country, King was born into a comfortable, privileged setting. He was shielded from the economic depression that developed less than a year after his birth. Not long after he joined the church at the age of five (because his sister had done so), says Stephen Oates, his father "officially corrected both their names to Martin Luther King, Sr. and Jr."[1]

King was a normal child who grew up in a middle-class environment. His parents stressed hard work, thrift, saving, service to others, and upward mobility. They also stressed the importance of education, responsibility, and sacrifice. King's childhood was marked by "order, balance, and restraint."[2] However, unlike in many white middle-class families, King and his siblings were not taught to despise people solely because of their race.

Sundays in the King home were devoted to church. Furthermore, each day began and ended with family prayers, and the children were required to learn and recite passages of Scripture at the dinner table. King had a paper route, less to earn money than for discipline and developing the habit of work.

Fundamentalist teachings regarding the Bible were basically conveyed to King and other Ebenezer Baptist Church youth by Sunday school teachers and through his father's sermons. They were taught the inerrancy and infallibility of the Bible, as well as the truth of the virgin birth and the bodily resurrection of Jesus. Youth were not permitted to question these or any other orthodox Christian teachings. However, by age thirteen King was already doing just that. For example, he doubted the truth of the literal bodily resurrection of Jesus. He recalled growing increasingly "skeptical of Sunday-school Christianity" and was embarrassed by the "unbridled emotionalism" in his father's church. These were the types of things that initially led King to reject ministry as the best means of helping his father fight racism and discrimination.

Martin Luther King Jr. was an ordinary human being who, because of his faith and deep love for God and human beings, did some very extraordinary things. It is important to remember this if we are to understand King as a man of consummate ideas and social activism who tried to actualize the beloved community—that thoroughly integrated community in which every person, regardless of race, gender, sexuality, class, or age will be respected and treated humanely. It is a community characterized throughout by shared power.

As armchair theologians, we will understand King best as a theological social ethicist when we consider these questions: What was the nature of his heritage, family, and educational background? What were some of the formative ideas from his familial and church upbringing that became important in his theological development and his social activism? What did he learn from his parents and grandparents about the expectations of Christians? What did he learn from them about the social gospel and prophetic ministry? Was there evidence of leanings toward nonviolent direct action in King's family history?

In this chapter we will see that a number of King's most important theological and ethical ideas are rooted in the teachings of his family and church, as well as the ministries of his parents and grandparents. King was, to the very end, a man of ideas and social activism, as well as a man of the South. Moreover, he was faithful to his calling, right up to the time that a bullet slug ended his life on earth.

Martin Luther King acknowledged that his religious ideas were shaped by his childhood experiences and beliefs. These included (1) the warm and loving home environment provided by his parents; (2) the intimate love of his parents for each other and for their three children; (3) financial security and living in a relatively safe, low-crime area; (4) a dear and loving maternal grandmother; (5) the primacy of church, which King referred to as "a second home"; (6) fundamentalist religious beliefs that shaped his

early religious ideas until he rejected them beginning at age thirteen; (7) an early belief in personal immortality or life after death, as a result of explanations by his parents regarding the status of his deceased maternal grandmother; and (8) early encounters with racism, and his parents' relentless counsel that Christianity required that he love even the white man who despitefully used and persecuted him and his people because of their race. These and other childhood and adolescent experiences and ideas prepared King's mind for his encounter with the liberal theological ideas he studied in college, seminary, and during doctoral studies.

King was the son, grandson, and great-grandson of southern black Baptist preachers. His brother and one of their paternal uncles were also Baptist preachers. King concluded that he did not have much choice but to be a preacher. In fact, despite his leadership in the civil and human rights movements and all of the awards he received, King declared in 1967 that ministry was both his first calling and his "greatest commitment." So imbued was he with ministry that he said everything he did was done because of his sense that it was part of his ministry. King was, first and foremost, a Baptist preacher. Ministry was the vocation to which he was most deeply devoted. A look at King's family roots will provide a foundation for understanding his deep commitment to ministry, as well as his emphasis on thought and social activism.

Paternal Grandfather: James Albert King

James Albert King (1864–1933) was the son of an enslaved Afrikan and was himself a sharecropper in Stockbridge, Georgia, during the 1880s. The white plantation owner provided King and his family many of the necessities for survival, but in a way that guaranteed his constant indebtedness. The owner did not hesitate to take advantage of the

illiterate King, who also lacked mathematical skills. Therefore, King worked from sunup to sundown and still owed the owner at the end of the year.

In his youth, James King was a hard and tireless worker in a dead-end job. His sense of worth as a human being slowly faded, and he turned to heavy drinking. His wife, on the other hand, found comfort and solace in religion.

James Albert King and Delia King were the parents of ten children, one of whom died in infancy. Census records suggest that the second born and the first son of the King children was "probably" born on December 19, 1897. His mother wanted to name him Michael, after the archangel. His father wanted to name him after his two brothers, Martin and Luther. A compromise was reached, and he was called "Mike." Years later, on his deathbed, James King asked his son (Mike) to officially change his name to Martin Luther, which he did. Mike also changed his son's name to Martin Luther King Jr.

The relationship between James King and his son was a volatile one, due largely to the father's heavy drinking and his tendency to be abusive toward his wife. As the oldest son, Mike could not permit this, and thus father and son sometimes got physical over the matter. In a drunken state the elder King was no match for his powerfully built teenage son.

Mike King remained on the Stockbridge plantation until the age of sixteen, when he decided he could no longer put up with sharecropping and the dehumanization that came with it. Moreover, having been taught by his religious mother the virtue of honoring his parents, he no longer wanted to be around to fight with his father. He therefore packed his meager belongings and headed for Atlanta.

Paternal Grandmother: Delia King

Delia King was a woman of deep religious faith who lived by the conviction that God will make a way out of no way. Her religious faith offered at least a modicum of relief from the hardships of sharecropping and doing domestic work in the homes of white women. Her faith in God enabled her to be "at peace with herself . . . even in her times of great suffering,"[3] said Mike King.

Delia King had a generally subdued temper, unlike her husband. Although she loved her children dearly, she was a strict disciplinarian who expected them to be mindful of their sense of values and to obey her at all times. It usually took something major to upset her to the point of losing her temper. Whenever this happened, Mike King recalled, it usually meant big trouble for the one who caused it.

Protective of her children, Delia King did not hesitate to let this be known, even to whites. This is an important point, for it reveals the importance on both sides of King Jr.'s family of the will to fight to preserve and enhance one's dignity. In any case, when it came to protecting her children, Delia King's response was not always of the non-violent type.

A story reveals Delia King's commitment to the spirit of racial uplift and dignity, and a willingness to resort to violence if necessary. When Mike King was around twelve years of age he was severely beaten by the local sawmill owner while on an errand for his mother. King recalled that when he arrived home bloodied, his mother was furious when he told her what happened. She took her son and confronted the mill owner. His attempt to intimidate her failed, and she pounced on him, took him to the ground, and pounded his face with her fists. She then told the man that he could do what he wanted to her, but he would answer to her if he ever again touched one of her children. This was a very dangerous act on the part of Delia King, since in those days blacks were lynched for much less. What is important is that Delia King's action exhibited the spirit of protest, part of her legacy to her paternal grandson.

However, when we look for the family roots of King Jr.'s ethic of nonviolence, we should not look to his paternal grandparents or to his father (who possessed a volatile temper). What we do find in these paternal family members, however, is a strong determination to protest the wrongdoing and injustices committed by whites. This legacy of impassioned protest and determination was passed on to King Jr.

Maternal Grandfather: Adam Daniel Williams

Willis Williams (1810–?), was an old-time enslaved Baptist preacher. He married Lucrecia Daniel (1840–?), and the couple gave birth to five children. One was Adam Daniel Williams (hereafter A. D., 1863–1931), King Jr.'s maternal grandfather. Having undergone a religious conversion, followed by baptism in the summer of 1884, A. D. was aided by his pastor in preparing for ministry. He was licensed to preach in 1888, and within five years he migrated to Atlanta.

Serving as pastor for two small Baptist churches for a brief period, Williams was called in March 1894 to pastor Ebenezer Baptist Church, founded by Reverend John Andrew Parker (who had recently died). The church had a membership of thirteen, and there was no building. However, the energetic, enterprising, committed, entrepreneurial, and creative Williams was not discouraged. By the end of his first year as pastor, sixty-five new members had joined. Before long the church was prospering as a result of his recipe for building a strong congregation and ministry. This included "forceful preaching" that stressed the humanity and everyday needs and struggles of the members. Williams was committed early to social gospel Christianity—applying the Christian gospel to eliminating social problems. He also knew the value of education and therefore sought to overcome some of his own deficiencies by enrolling in Atlanta Baptist College.

Williams met and soon married Jennie Celeste Parks, daughter of William and Fannie Parks. She was one of thirteen children and attended Spelman Seminary, although she did not graduate. Considered a deeply pious and spiritual woman, she was thought by many to be the quintessential minister's wife. On September 13, 1903, they gave birth to their sole surviving child, Alberta Christine Williams, the mother of King Jr.

Because of his intellect, vast experience, and amazingly practical ways in conveying the Christian gospel, A. D. Williams became a leader among his ministerial peers. By the end of 1903, Ebenezer's membership had grown to approximately four hundred. He was a pioneer in advocating "a distinctive African-American version of the social gospel, endorsing a strategy that combined elements of [Booker T.] Washington's emphasis on black business development and W. E. B. DuBois' call for civil rights activism."[4]

Since social gospel Christianity was a chief characteristic in the ministries of King Jr.'s father and grandfather, it is reasonable to conclude that King Jr. at least gained through them an *informal* theological rationale for doing social gospel ministry. This preseminary theological rationale was shaped by the sermons and social witness of his father, grandfather, and other southern black preachers in the tradition of black social gospelism.[5] These included William Holmes Borders, pastor of the famous Wheat Street Baptist Church in Atlanta, as well as King Jr.'s pastor-scholar teachers at Morehouse College such as George Kelsey, Benjamin Mays, and Samuel Williams.

A. D. Williams was a charter member and president of the local chapter of the NAACP in Atlanta in 1917. Earlier he joined over five hundred black Georgians, including religious, civic, and educational leaders, to form the Georgia Equal Rights League in February 1906, in order to challenge the barring of blacks from participation in the Democratic primary. His leadership and involvement in such organized social protests points to the deep roots of social protest and social gospel Christianity in King Jr.'s family lineage.

Maternal Grandmother: Jennie Celeste Williams

Like Delia King, Jennie Celeste (Parks) Williams (1873–1941), the maternal grandmother of King Jr., was a devoutly religious person. Of a different spirit, personality, and social class than Delia King, she was more inclined to the nonviolent spirit of protest. As the pastor's wife, she had considerable influence at Ebenezer Baptist Church.

King Jr. was two years old when A. D. Williams died. Mike King was appointed pastor of Ebenezer to a large extent because of Jennie Williams, who lived with the Kings until her death about ten years later. The relationship between Jennie Williams and King Jr. was especially close. In addition, she contributed much toward teaching him and his siblings important family, religious, and cultural values, frequently using storytelling as the teaching medium.

The role of Jennie Williams in the King household echoed that of the black grandmother during the period of American enslavement. She was a deep repository of black experience, memory, culture, spiritual strength, and wisdom that provided continuity to the new generations. King Jr. learned much from his grandmother about the ministry and social activism of A. D. Williams.

Contributions of King Jr.'s Parents

Mike King (hereafter Daddy King) was an eager and industrious youth who was steeped in fundamentalist Christian faith. He worked long, hard hours once he left the Stockbridge plantation and settled in Atlanta. He was frugal, saved most of his money, studied, and attended school at night. After graduating from high school, he was relentless in his effort to gain even conditional admission to More-house College.

While attending Morehouse, Daddy King was pastor of two small churches in Atlanta. He soon met Alberta Williams, whose father had a reputation for courageously standing up to white people. In addition, A. D. Williams had the well-deserved reputation for being able to accu-mulate material wealth, and he became one of black Atlanta's elite, a point that was not lost on Daddy King.

Daddy King was much influenced by Williams's style of ministry and his concern for the poor and oppressed of his race. Even before Daddy King was ordained he already understood and took as his own the idea that it is the pas-tor's obligation and responsibility to minister to the every-day needs of church members. As a youngster, Daddy King had much respect for those black preachers who stood up to whites and did not soften their prophetic critique of racism.

Alberta Williams and Daddy King were married on November 25, 1926. A. D. Williams persuaded King to be his associate pastor at Ebenezer. He remained in that capacity until Williams died five years later in 1931. Shortly thereafter, Daddy King became the senior minister.

A member of the black elite and ruling class of Atlanta, Daddy King, says Lerone Bennett Jr., was also "among the pioneer leaders of the modern Negro resistance move-ment."[6] The spirit of protest was prevalent on both sides of King Jr.'s family. This is an important point in the family background of one who was part and parcel of the soil of black Christian social gospel activism.

King Jr. remembered Daddy King's telling him as a boy that he would never accept racism and segregation but would fight against them as long as he lived. Although he did not fully understand what his father meant, the boy promised that he would do all he could to help him. King Jr. recalled that he had never seen his father so angry as when a white shoe salesman refused to wait on him in the front of the store. Just like his own parents before him, Daddy King protested against acts of racial injustice as best he could, never hesitating to stand up for his dignity and rights.

Because of this, King Jr. credited his father with doing much to shape his social conscience. Daddy King had been president of the Atlanta chapter of the NAACP, and he courageously challenged injustice. He refused to ride segregated buses and fought to equalize the pay of white and black school teachers in Atlanta. King Jr.'s admiration for his father's social gospel ministry was an important factor in his decision to answer the call to ministry. Although seminary would give him the formal education, his father and others in the black church tradition supplied him with models for actually doing social gospel ministry based on their understanding of the Christian faith.

The strength, intimacy, and love that King Jr.'s parents had for each other and for their three children instilled in the children a sense of stability, safety, and security. Theirs was a traditional family, with the father as "the head of the house" who provided for the family financially, while the mother was the primary caregiver to all members. Although Daddy King was the primary disciplinarian and could be very strict, he could also be very compassionate in his parenting.

Both of King Jr.'s parents were committed to instilling in him and his siblings a strong sense of self and somebodyness, as well as the value of acknowledging and respecting the humanity and dignity of others. Such teachings, along with the belief in a personal and infinitely loving God, were the bases of King's *homespun personalism* (explored in the next chapter). The King children also learned much from their parents about the need to be self-determined and in control of their own destiny, despite conditions such as racism.

When the parents of a white friend of six-year-old King Jr. told King he could no longer play with their son because he was "a Negro," he began to cry and ran home. Once there, his mother explained to him what every caring and loving black parent has to explain to her children. She gave him a history lesson, explaining that his ancestors were Afrikans who were forced into enslavement in the Americas by white men. She explained the system of segregation and the meaning of racial discrimination, and then she told the boy what so many black parents of that period had to tell their children, namely, that he "was as good as anybody."

This was but one example of both the tender and forceful influence that King's mother had on him. Lewis V. Baldwin rightly contends that this early counsel "must have been important in laying a foundation for the abiding faith,

optimism, and self-confidence which King later displayed in his efforts to transform and regenerate human society."[7] Just as Daddy King's mother had urged him from her deathbed not to hate all white people, Alberta Williams and Daddy King reminded their son that Christianity does not permit the hatred of any persons. Although King remembered coming "perilously close to resenting all white people,"[8] this sentiment subsided during his experience in the interracial Intercollegiate Council that he participated in while at Morehouse. From that experience he learned that not all whites were as racist as many of those he had encountered, and that some, especially youth, sought to be allies.

Possibly more than anyone else, King Jr.'s mother shaped his sense of morality by instilling in him three things: (1) the sense of the strict Baptist moral code, which primarily stressed personal morality, such as avoiding drinking, smoking, premarital sex, and dancing; (2) the sense that he was somebody; and (3) the sense of the power and duty of Christian love.[9] The last two of these remained as central influences throughout King's adult life.

The incident regarding King's white friend was traumatic, but he also remembered being slapped by a white woman in a downtown Atlanta store. He recalled that "the only thing I heard was somebody saying, 'You are that nigger that stepped on my foot.' "[10] Although only eight years of age, he knew instinctively that he could not retaliate, for it could mean severe consequences for him and/or his parents. But, interestingly, looking back he said that in part he did not retaliate because "it was part of my native structure—that is, that I have never been one to hit back."[11] Perhaps this was a result of the spirit of nonviolence passed on to him by his mother. Another of his early contacts with the practice of nonviolent resistance to social evil was through observing his father's Christian social activism and efforts to organize blacks to protest nonviolently against injustice.

Marriage and Career Ideas

Martin Luther King Jr. met Coretta Scott in 1952 while she was a student at the New England Conservatory of Music in Boston and he was a doctoral student at Boston

University. Scott had no intention of marrying a preacher, since many of the ones she knew were fundamentalist, pompous, and narrow in their religious thinking. How could she possibly marry a minister? King was successful in easing her concerns.

According to Scott, she and King spent considerable time discussing what type of marriage they wanted and what each desired in a spouse. King wanted a woman who would be a good wife and mother to their children, and be at home to greet him when his workday ended. He also desired a mate who was intelligent and could think for herself. Scott had these and other traits that appealed to him. However, King also believed the man should be the head of the family.

Although Coretta King said that she later resigned herself to be the supportive wife she thought her husband needed, she continued to be her own person and to think and speak her own thoughts. In addition, while she wrote of the importance of black men assuming "their natural place as the head of the household and the protector of their families," she did not hesitate to refer to the limits of this.[12] In her thinking, headship did not mean that she was to be uncritically submissive and obedient to her husband. This may be why they asked Daddy King (who performed their wedding on June 18, 1953) to leave out the phrase about the bride obeying her husband.

Although King had thoughts of teaching at a college or seminary after earning his PhD at Boston University—and received a number of offers to do so—he also felt a strong inclination to pastor a church in his beloved South. He did not forget his boyhood promise to help his father fight racism.

CHAPTER THREE

Ideas from the Academy

While in high school King rejected the ministry. He had grown up with fundamentalist teachings and what he perceived as too much emotionalism in worship services. He wondered "whether religion could be intellectually respectable as well as emotionally satisfying."[1] When he came under the influence of President Mays and Professor Kelsey at Morehouse College, he saw ministry and the minister in a much more favorable light.

Kelsey challenged King to look behind the myths in the Bible stories to get at the deep abiding truths that many of them contained. He was inspired by Kelsey's belief that modern times called for ministers who were well educated *and* committed to social Christianity. King was grateful to Kelsey for removing "the shackles of fundamentalism" from him.

Not unlike Kelsey, Mays modeled for King the true minister, described by Stephen Oates as "a rational man whose sermons were both spiritually and intellectually stimulating, a moral man who was socially involved."[2] King's ideal of the minister was one who is intellectually astute and invigorating, and one who strives to live by and apply the ethical ideals of the Jewish and Christian faiths to the social struggle.

Martin Luther King accepted the call to ministry during his last year in college. After his exposure to the more liberal theological ideas of Mays, Kelsey, Walter Chivers, and Samuel Williams, it seemed only natural that he would want a more liberal theological education in preparation for ministry. To this end he chose Crozer Theological Seminary in Chester, Pennsylvania.

This chapter examines some of the important ideas that King studied from college through graduate school. His first introduction to a number of these ideas occurred during his family and church upbringing and his experience at Morehouse, ideas such as his belief in an objective moral order and his sense of the depth of human sinfulness. When he entered Morehouse College at age fifteen, he was already primed to look critically at his religious beliefs.

There are a number of ideas that King thought about before he entered seminary. I refer to these as *homespun* ideas, meaning that he heard some form of them in sermons, speeches, and lectures given by his father and other black preachers, as well as his Morehouse pastor-scholar teachers, before he was formally introduced to them in seminary. These ideas include his sense of the strong social

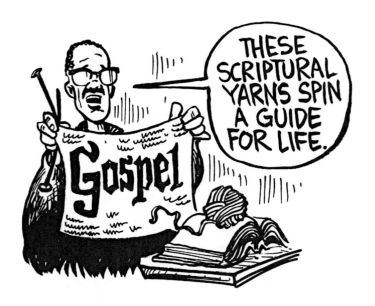

gospel and the prophetic element in ministry, and his conviction that there are immutable moral laws that govern the universe. Although these and other ideas have a homespun character, they each received a formal theological and philosophical basis in seminary and graduate school.

The great contribution of King's Morehouse teachers was that they directed him on the road to *thinking* about his faith claims and their socioethical implications for ministry. His teachers at Crozer went further by impressing upon him the importance of thinking theologically (*theos* = God; ology = *study of*). For our purpose, *theology* means the critical study of God and the mutual relationship between God, human beings, other life forms, and the world. King's personalist teachers and mentors at Boston University helped to deepen his understanding of the philosophy of personalism and its implications for social activism.

In the two versions of his intellectual autobiography

called *Pilgrimage to Nonviolence* (1958 and 1963), King discusses aspects of his formal intellectual journey through seminary and graduate studies.[3] My purpose is not to reproduce what King has already done in those documents. Rather, I want to discuss the meaning of several of the key theological and philosophical ideas he studied and how he reacted to them.

By the time King entered Morehouse College he already possessed by his own account a substantial "concern for racial and economic justice."[4] While in seminary he hoped to accomplish two things: to find a formal theological rationale on which to ground his social conscience, and to discover a method to address and eradicate racism and other social evils. The social gospel writings of Walter Rauschenbusch (1861–1918) provided the formal theological rationale. Mohandas K. Gandhi's philosophy of nonviolence supplied the method, although King was not at that time a Gandhian.

What follows is a cursory treatment of five theological and philosophical ideas that were influential in King's formal intellectual development and that later significantly influenced his social activism: (1) objective moral order, (2) Hegel and dialectical thinking, (3) the social gospel, (4) Niebuhr and sin, and (5) personalism. He received formal instruction on these ideas in seminary and at Boston University.

Objective Moral Order

The conviction that there is an objective moral order in creation is the fundamental principle on which King's entire theological social ethics and his doctrine of nonviolent resistance to evil are built. This conviction holds that the universe is founded on goodness or morality. In addi-

tion to the present discussion, we will revisit objective moral order in the discussion on nonviolence in chapter 5.

To make an objective claim about something is to suggest that it exists and is relevant independent of the person making the claim. It is given and is discoverable by any disciplined, rational mind. The claim that there are objective moral laws such as the law of love, for example, means that they exist and are relevant to human beings whether a given human being is aware of their existence or not.

Most likely Benjamin E. Mays introduced King to this idea at Morehouse. In *Seeking to Be Christian in Race Relations*, Mays wrote, "Christianity declares that the universe is essentially ethical and essentially moral."[5] The world is fundamentally moral and good because this is the way God constructed it. This implies that there are certain moral laws by which we should seek to live, just as there are certain physical laws—such as the law of gravity—that govern or regulate the universe. According to Mays, human beings no more create the moral laws that govern human behavior than the physical laws that govern nature. Both have their source in God. The task of human beings is to discover the moral laws of God and devote all their might to living in accordance with them. When King declared in his senior sermon at Morehouse that "there are moral laws of the universe that man can no more violate with impunity than he can violate its physical laws,"[6] he was very likely influenced by Mays. King often said that the universe hinges on a moral foundation. In a related sense, he frequently quoted the nineteenth-century preacher-abolitionist Theodore Parker: "The arc of the moral universe is long, but it bends toward justice." This may be interpreted to mean that because the universe is fused with value, justice will ultimately overtake the forces of injustice.

This conviction strengthened King's faith that Easter will come after the tragedy of Good Friday, for Easter is a reminder that "God ultimately rules history" and that "the forces of evil and injustice cannot survive."[7] Furthermore, this belief that the universe is infused with value allowed King to keep theology and ethics together. What was always at issue for King was not merely that there is a supreme power working in the universe, but that this power created the world out of love for the good of all. Such a view convinced King that through human and divine cooperative endeavor, social evil and injustice will ultimately give way to good and justice. The God of the Hebrew prophets and Jesus Christ is not only supremely powerful but also supremely good. This is why King insisted that the universe has a moral foundation and that theology (what we think about God) and ethics (what we do in light of our conception of God) must be integrally related.

Hegel and Dialectical Thinking

As a doctoral student at Boston University, King took a one-year seminar on the philosophy of Hegel (1770–1831). He took at least two things from Hegel that influenced his thinking and ministerial practice. First, King much appreciated Hegel's dictum that "the truth is the whole."[8] In any honest search for truth one must examine all of the available relevant data and devise the most reasonable and coherent view. Throughout his ministry it was a common practice for King to examine all relevant sides of an issue before coming to a decision about steps to be taken. Indeed, this practice often led to the criticism that he was indecisive regarding next steps in some of the civil rights campaigns. Frequently, however, he was simply examining all sides of the issue, and this took time.

Second, despite its shortcomings, King was impressed with Hegel's analysis of the dialectical process. Hegel saw this process at work in reason, history, and the universe as a whole. Simply put, the dialectical process entails a necessary

movement from thesis to antithesis, and then to a synthesis of the two. Since this process rejects the "either-or" approach in favor of the "both-and" approach, it allowed King to see that some truth, however miniscule it may be at times, may exist in quite opposite ideas or viewpoints, and that taken together one may arrive at a fuller, more reasonable view of truth—that is, a synthesis of the strong points in the two opposites. To put it another way, one may be able to arrive at a middle or compromise position, which King often did in his civil rights ministry.

One can see King's use of this Hegelian principle in many of his speeches, sermons, writings, and interviews. For example, in his article "The 'New Negro' of the South: Behind the Montgomery Story" (1956), King examined the question of progress in race relations, contending that there were three ways to think about progress: *extreme optimism, extreme pessimism,* and *the realistic stance.* He examined the strengths and limitations of the first two and concluded that the more reasonable position is the third, since it incorporates the truths of the other two. "Like the synthesis of Hegelian philosophy," King said, "the realistic attitude seeks to reconcile the truths of two opposites and avoid the extremes of both. So the realist in race relations would agree with the optimist in saying, we have come a long way, but he would balance that by agreeing with the pessimist that we have a long way to go."[9]

According to King, the dialectical process also enables one to see that struggle is often involved in the search for truth, as well as the search for freedom. Indeed, Hegel said that "it is solely by risking life that freedom is obtained."[10] King also appealed to Hegel's doctrine that growth comes through struggle: "It is both historically and biologically true," King said, "that there can be no birth and growth without . . . growing pains."[11]

Social Gospel

Although King received a good dose of social gospel teachings under Mays, Kelsey, and Williams at Morehouse, his first formal systematic reading of social gospel literature occurred in seminary. Indeed, even before King read social gospel literature he declared in a paper in a preaching class during his very first semester, "I am a profound advocate of the social gospel."[12] King's study of white social gospelism differed from what he experienced from social gospel practitioners in the black church tradition, not least his father and maternal grandfather. Unlike their white

counterparts, blacks did not have the luxury of merely *proclaiming* the doctrine of Christian social responsibility and the need for activism based on Christian principles. Instead, they had to *do* social gospel ministry, both because it was God's mandate and because they and their people were in the belly of the beast.

King studied several basic traits of the social gospel in seminary. First, proponents generally believed that the social and ethical principles of Jesus, such as his emphasis on the coming of the kingdom of God, were good guides for the behavior of individuals and groups of all kinds. The belief in progress was a second basic trait of the social gospel. King was primarily influenced by the social gospel teachings of Walter Rauschenbusch. However, King criticized Rauschenbusch because he believed that he "had fallen victim to the nineteenth-century 'cult of inevitable progress' which led him to a superficial optimism concerning man's nature."[13] King concluded that progress in the social order is anything but inevitable. Progress comes because of relentless human initiative and cooperative endeavor between human beings and God.

Belief in the goodness of human nature is a third theme of the social gospel. Rauschenbusch qualified this belief with his realism, that is, his strong sense of humans' propensity to sin—individually and corporately. Closely related, King's social gospelism was qualified by his homespun realism and the realism of Reinhold Niebuhr. From each he developed a deep belief in the prevalence and depth of sin in individual and corporate relations. A fourth theme of the social gospel was its emphasis on the Christian love ethic and the sense that by following this imperative individuals and groups could do much to actualize the kingdom of God on earth.

Reinhold Niebuhr and Sin

Various experiences King had growing up in the Deep South influenced his understanding of human nature and kept him from uncritically accepting the liberal theological emphasis on humans' fundamental goodness. King's view of human nature was influenced by his homespun realism. In a paper written during his second year of seminary, King grappled with how to think of human nature. He was at a transitional period, struggling with both neo-orthodox and liberal stances, and for the first time he wrote formally of the role of some of the ugly things he had experienced regarding race in the South. "At one time I find myself leaning toward a mild neo-orthodox view of

man." He went on to say that this "may root back to certain experiences that I had in the south with a vicious race problem. Some of the experiences that I encountered there made it very difficult for me to believe in the essential goodness of man."[14]

We should not underestimate the contributions of the realism—political and theological—of King's teachers at Morehouse.[15] For example, his academic advisor was Walter Chivers. As a political realist Chivers was suspicious of those who espoused views of the dignity of persons at the expense of acknowledging and fighting to eliminate the racism embedded in the American social system. Chivers surely talked in his classes about a retarding factor in human groups that made it difficult for them to see others as they saw themselves, a point that would not have escaped King's attention. In courses under Kelsey and Williams, King was further exposed to realistic ideas about human nature and the political system.

Reinhold Niebuhr (1892–1971) is often labeled as a neo-orthodox theologian, although early in his career he had been in the ranks of liberal social gospel theologians. Liberal theology dates back to Friedrich Schleiermacher (1768–1834) and sought to reinterpret Christian doctrine in contemporary terms through stressing the use of reason, human freedom, science, and experience. Proponents emphasized the inherent goodness of human nature, progress, and similarities between human and divine. The neo-orthodox revolt against this theology came to full bloom in Europe and the United States after World War II and continued to be prominent until the 1960s. Niebuhr was a chief proponent in the United States.

Neo-orthodox theology sought to reinterpret Reformation themes. Against liberal theology it asserted the utter transcendence and unknowableness of God, the prevalence of sin, and the absolute centrality of Jesus Christ. Niebuhr focused on the latter two themes.

King did not consider himself to be a neo-orthodox theologian. Even after his sharp criticism of liberal theology's failure to take sin seriously enough in its doctrine of human nature, he essentially remained in the liberal camp, vowing to always hold dear its emphasis on using reason, science, and freedom in the search for higher degrees of truth. For King these were among "the endearing qualities in liberalism," no matter what thunderous proclamations were made by fundamentalism and neo-orthodoxy. Because he took seriously the neo-orthodox critique of some aspects of liberalism, it is reasonable with Bernard Ramm to characterize King as "a liberal theologian with a neo-orthodox corrective."[16]

King began to read and study Niebuhr's works in his senior year of seminary, and he deepened that study at

Boston University. He appreciated Niebuhr's passionate style and his emphasis on the justice theme of the Hebrew prophets. However, King found Niebuhr's critique of Gandhi's doctrine of nonviolence to be less persuasive.

As King read Niebuhr and reflected on his own study of liberal theology, he came to the conclusion that liberalism's too optimistic view of human nature blinded it to "the fact that reason is darkened by sin."[17] His reading of Niebuhr, coupled with his experiences in the South, helped him to see clearly that liberalism had been much too optimistic regarding the goodness of human nature and that this needed to be tempered with an awareness of the prevalence and depth of sin, no matter how much progress is made.

King appreciated Niebuhr's emphasis on human sin, but he believed Niebuhr went too far by overcorrecting the liberal emphasis on the goodness of human nature. Appealing to the Hegelian method, King concluded that Niebuhr overemphasized the element of corruption in human nature, while liberalism overemphasized its inherent goodness. Acknowledging the element of truth in each position, King maintained that Niebuhr's "pessimism concerning human nature was not balanced by an optimism concerning divine nature. He was so involved in diagnosing man's sickness of sin that he overlooked the cure of grace."[18] This led King to conclude that true Christian realism "says that standing over against the tragic dimensions of man's sin is the glorious dimensions of God's grace. Where Sin abounded, grace abounded even more exceedingly."[19] This, King believed, avoids an otherwise "deadening pessimism" regarding human nature.[20] King's study of Niebuhr provided the formal theological foundation for his realistic view of human nature and his deepening appreciation for the place of sin in the relations of individuals and groups of all kinds.

Personalism

Home, church, and culture influenced King's acceptance of personalism, the theology or philosophy that the Creator God is personal and that persons are the highest intrinsic values.[21] Personalism also places a strong emphasis on the existence of an objective moral order, as well as the centrality of freedom. Personalism holds that to be a person is to be free, and to be free is to be a person.

As a child, King had frequent exposure to personalist ideas. His parents, grandmother, and Sunday school teachers taught him, his siblings, and peers that persons are

sacred before God because God created, loves, and imbues them—one and all—with the image of God. King's mother also taught him something about the value of human beings by insisting that he was to return love for hate. These were fundamental personalist ideas, but his mother couched such teachings in terms of what was required of Christians. In addition, King surely heard his father and other black ministers preach sermons in which they sought to build up a sense of worth and esteem in black church members. These Christian values were also basic tenets of personalism, although this fact was unknown to King's parents.

King acknowledged his debt to personalism, saying that it strengthened him in his two long-held convictions that God is personal, and persons possess inherent dignity. Personalism provided the philosophical framework for these convictions. Before King ever heard of personalism, these two beliefs were integral to his worldview. They were his Christian principles and convictions. King was just as comfortable speaking and writing about these principles in the language of personalism as he was in the language of Christianity and the Bible. One illustration of each must suffice.

Personalism was much influenced by Immanuel Kant's doctrine of persons as ends in themselves, which implies the inherent dignity of persons. One reason that King rejected segregation was that it "stands diametrically opposed to the principle of the sacredness of human personality." He appealed to Kant for support: "Immanuel Kant said . . . that 'all men must be treated as *ends* and never as mere *means*.' The tragedy of segregation is that it treats men as means rather than ends, and thereby reduces them to things rather than persons."[22]

Martin Luther King just as easily turned to Christian

and biblical language to express the same principle. Preaching on the parable of the Lost Sheep, he said that the parable "teaches the preciousness of the individual to God. . . . The Christian gospel is committed, once and for all, to the worth of the individual. By his cross, Christ has bound all men into an inextricably [*sic*] bond of brotherhood, and stamped on all men the indelible imprint of preciousness."[23]

This leads me to conclude that King was the quintessential *Christian social personalist*. More than any of his personalist teachers at Boston University, he led the way in applying and living personalist principles in the dangerous work of the civil rights movement. Before we explore how

King's theological, social, and ethical beliefs shaped his civil rights leadership, we turn in the next chapter to discuss the Montgomery bus boycott and some of the forerunners who prepared the way for his civil rights ministry.

CHAPTER FOUR

Montgomery

In addition to investigating the historic boycott of the Montgomery, Alabama, municipal bus system and the resulting fall of legal segregation, this chapter examines the contributions of some of the forerunners to the bus boycott—those who tilled the soil and prepared the way. These include Vernon Johns, Mary Fair Burks, Jo Ann Robinson, Claudette Colvin and Mary Louise Smith (both high school students), Rosa Parks, and Edwin D. Nixon. The boycott was not King's plan, nor had he been called to the

Dexter Avenue Baptist Church in Montgomery for the purpose of initiating and leading it. In fact, he initially hesitated to get directly involved, feeling that he needed more time to get to know the city and its centers of powers.

Much groundbreaking work had been done in Montgomery's black community that prepared the way for King's leadership, and we will learn about the specific contributions of some of the groundbreakers and their importance to the ensuing civil and human rights movements. Because the significance of their contributions was frequently downplayed until recent scholarship on King and the civil rights movement highlighted it, special attention is given here to the contributions of black women (and black youth in chapter 6).

Not long after King assumed full-time pastoral responsibilities at Dexter Avenue Baptist Church, a black seamstress, Rosa Parks, boarded a city bus to go home. It was to her just another Thursday afternoon. She was no more tired than usual. However, her fatigue was exacerbated by a sense of being sick of being tired and being mistreated. She followed the custom of sitting in the "Negro" section of the bus, although she was required by law and custom to relinquish her seat to any white passenger that wanted it. To add insult to injury, black patrons had to deposit their fare at the front of the bus, exit the bus, and reboard at the rear. On that particular Thursday afternoon, December 1, 1955, Rosa Parks had not planned to do anything different from what she had done hundreds of times when she boarded a city bus. When the bus driver stopped to pick up several white patrons and ordered the black passengers sitting just behind the "whites only" section to give up their seats, all did so except Parks, who simply slid into the window seat vacated by another black passenger.

Although physically tired, Rosa Parks was even more

tired of the humiliation that she and other black patrons—principally women who rode the buses to and from work—experienced as a result of the treatment of the bus drivers. Since she refused to give up her seat, custom and law required that the bus driver summon a police officer. Parks was immediately handcuffed and placed under arrest for failing to comply with the city's segregation codes.

There were many forces at work both before and during that fateful day. Unquestionably, the events leading up to and following the arrest of Parks were events whose time had come. It was not solely her arrest that caused the chain of events that followed. Much had already happened in

Montgomery. Much was in process of happening, not least a growing sense of utter frustration experienced by the black community over the segregation laws. Moreover, many black women in Montgomery were united against the bus segregation issue prior to Parks's arrest. They had already formulated plans to initiate a one-day bus boycott, even if the black male leadership of Montgomery refused to join them. Indeed, some students at the all-black Alabama State College in Montgomery had already initiated their own boycott of the city buses. Powerful forces—cosmic, divine, and human—had been at work for a long time in preparation for December 1, 1955.

Rosa Parks was not the first black person to be arrested for violating Montgomery's segregation ordinances. Numerous blacks had done this and were arrested. While the time is always ripe to do the right thing, the arrest of Rosa Parks and the swift reaction of Montgomery's black community was a reminder of how circumstances and events had converged to make December 1 the flashpoint for change.

Frequently history reveals how particular injustices may exist for long periods of time, and only after a confluence of events and forces is a movement mounted to eradicate them. This is what happened in Montgomery. It may be strange that the movement began only after Martin Luther King Jr. was called to be a minister in that city. King believed he had been "tracked down by the *Zeitgeist*" (the spirit of the times).[1] Much that had been happening in Montgomery long before his arrival helped prepare the way for his role as pastor of Dexter Avenue Baptist Church and later as leader of the Montgomery bus boycott. So before focusing on the bus boycott, we turn to one of the most important of those who prepared the way.

Vernon Johns: "God's Bad Boy"

Few played a more significant role in breaking ground for King and what came to be the civil rights movement than the venerable, albeit eccentric, Vernon Johns (1892–1965). He was born and reared on a farm in Farmville, Virginia, and was always a farmer at heart. He possessed a brilliant mind and was a scholar-preacher, trained in liberal theological ideas at Oberlin Seminary in Ohio. After graduation Johns enrolled in the Divinity School at the University of Chicago, a seedbed of social gospel liberalism. His solid religious scholarship and his strong, passionate preaching opened a number of employment possibilities for him. However, his temperament was such that he was seldom in any one place for too long.

Vernon Johns was as the prophets of old, declaring fearlessly what the Lord says about the need to do justice, love mercy, and walk humbly with God (Micah 6:8). Perhaps Charles Emerson Boddie said it best: "As John the Baptist was 'the voice of one crying in the wilderness, make straight the way of the Lord,' Vernon Johns fallowed the ground which provided the seedbed for the germination of the great movement led by another, whose name was Martin Luther King, Jr. . . . The martyred leader's ministry was found acceptable largely because Vernon Johns had already passed that way."[2]

God is *never* without a witness in history. Every witness has a role to play in the movement toward the realization of God's purposes in the world. Vernon Johns does not often get the recognition given King. However, without the commitment and obedience to God exhibited by Johns and many other lesser-known persons in Montgomery, there might not have been a massive bus boycott there in 1955.

History evolves and builds on what has gone before. Consequently, King inherited a sound protest tradition not only from his parents, grandparents, and teachers at Morehouse College, but from his predecessor at Dexter Avenue Baptist Church. Although Johns's tenure at Dexter lasted only four years (1948–1952), he was a true prophet in the tradition of Amos and Micah. It was the prophet in Johns—his staunch insistence that justice be done to black people—that kept him in hot water with the primarily black middle class members of Dexter and the white authorities of Montgomery. Johns also stressed the spirit of self-determination and economic freedom in his people.

Vernon Johns himself had an incident on a city bus. He paid his fare but refused to leave the bus and reenter from the rear. He simply paid the fare, took a seat, and refused to move. When the driver refused to put the bus in gear, Johns finally said that he would not ride the bus, and he even managed to get his money back, itself an amazing feat at that time. His was a one-man boycott of the city buses.

Just as Vernon Johns did not let whites off the moral hook, neither was he soft with his congregation and other members of the black community. Johns was without peer in preaching prophetic sermons on God's expectation that justice be done in righteous ways. He courageously related this to blacks' condition in Montgomery and did everything he could to rock the complacency of the refined members of Dexter. Considering that they were in Montgomery, Alabama, where blacks were frequent victims of racial violence, they had good reason to want their pastor to tone down his sermons. Nevertheless, a few members,

such as Mary Fair Burks and Jo Ann Robinson (whom we will meet shortly), were made of sterner stuff and were positively influenced by their pastor's bold sermons.

Unquestionably, Johns was the prophet's prophet. He did not refer to himself as a prophet, but he acted like one. He was truly one of "God's bad boys," in the sense that he not only could tell the gospel story but was adamant about applying it to both church and world while insisting that these come into line with *what the Lord says*. None was more committed to social gospelism than Vernon Johns. King himself was much influenced by this witness. In addition, Johns insisted on freedom to speak God's truth as he understood it, a trait that King took as his own.

Johns laid a sound social protest foundation for his immediate successor at Dexter. In this, he was without question the forerunner to King and what came to be known as *the movement*, and he was without peer in paving the way for the social activist ministry of King. Above all else, Vernon Johns demanded that justice be done and that racism in all its forms be eradicated forthwith. He saw love as the ultimate Christian imperative but was adamant that justice must be done first and foremost. God, for Vernon Johns, could not be the God of love and not require that justice be done to oppressed people.

Black Women Trailblazers

Rosa Parks was a seamstress at a local department store in Montgomery and the assistant to E. D. Nixon, president of the local chapter of the NAACP. She was devoted to civil rights for her people. After news of her arrest spread throughout the black community, black women decided that enough was enough. They already had in place an organization that could mobilize people against this most

recent assault on black personhood in general and black womanhood in particular. The Women's Political Council (WPC) was founded in 1951 by Mary Fair Burks, a faculty member at the all-black Alabama State College. The WPC was a response to the refusal of the League of Women Voters in Montgomery to admit black women. Burks, a member of Dexter Avenue Baptist Church during the tenure of Johns and King, reportedly got inspiration from a Johns sermon in 1946 to organize and move forward.

Under the leadership of Jo Ann Robinson, also a faculty member at Alabama State College, and Burks's successor as president of the WPC, the idea of a one-day boycott of the buses was conceived. When Robinson became president of the WPC her primary goal was to desegregate the buses, for she herself had been rudely treated by a bus driver. Like Burks and some others in the WPC, Robinson was also a member of the Social and Political Action Committee at Dexter, a committee that King had established. Jo Ann Robinson was astute and exhibited real political savvy, a point that King acknowledged. For instance, when trying to resolve the boycott, representatives of the Montgomery Improvement Association (MIA) and the bus company met with the mayor, who initially tried to stack the working committee with eight white men.[3] Then he permitted a total of five blacks, two of which he had chosen. It was Robinson who insisted on the need for equal representa-

tion on the committee. The mayor conceded, albeit reluctantly. By December 1955 no black organization in Montgomery was as organized and powerful as the Women's Political Council.

Certain actions of the WPC actually anticipated the Montgomery bus boycott by at least a year and a half. For example, on May 21, 1954, Jo Ann Robinson composed a letter on behalf of the WPC and sent it to Mayor W. A. Gayle. Although the letter did not challenge the state's segregation code, it reminded the mayor that three-fourths of those who rode the city buses were black, and that without their patronage the bus company could not remain in business. It was therefore good business sense to work toward more humane and respectful treatment of black passengers. The WPC wanted only that black passengers be treated with the same degree of respect as their white counterparts, and that the bus drivers honor the law. Separate but equal treatment—the law—is what they desired. This had been the law since the landmark case of *Plessy v. Ferguson* in 1896. In *Brown v. Board of Education of Topeka* the Supreme Court overturned *Plessy* on May 17, 1954 (four days before Robinson sent the letter to Mayor Gayle).

Most of the women in the WPC had actually wanted to boycott after fifteen-year-old Claudette Colvin was arrested and roughed up by police on March 2, 1955, for refusing to give up her bus seat. A very intelligent high school student who wanted to become a lawyer in order to help her people, Colvin was on her way home from school. When she refused to give her seat to a white patron, the police were summoned and she was forcibly removed from the bus. The women in the WPC, although furious, were dissuaded from launching a boycott at that time, but not without reluctance. E. D. Nixon, one of the black male

71

leaders, argued that because Colvin was single and preg-
nant, from a moral standpoint she was not a good test case
for the courts.

Some of the women, especially Robinson and Burks,
seethed with anger about this reaction on the part of
the black male leadership and insisted that it was not
Claudette Colvin's morality that was at issue but that of the
bus company, city officials, and the white community of
Montgomery. Neither was the issue whether some other
young woman's father was a drunk. The reference here is to
eighteen-year-old Mary Louise Smith, who was arrested in
October 1955, barely two months before the arrest of Rosa
Parks. Male leaders believed Smith's was not a good test
case either, since her father had a reputation for drinking
heavily. Smith and Colvin became two of four black women
plaintiffs to file a federal lawsuit (the decisive *Browder v.
Gayle* case) against Montgomery and the state of Alabama's
bus segregation statute. The women of the WPC had
grown weary of the black male leadership's imposed crite-
rion of finding the perfect judicial test case. They contended
that those who were being subjected to dehumanizing
treatment most—namely, black women—should be the
ones to decide when, where, and how to protest and resist.

More than a few black women in Montgomery shared
the sentiment of Gladys Moore when she talked about the
role of women in the boycott and who actually started it.
"Wasn't no man started it," she said. "We all started it over
night."[4] Moore herself had experienced abusive treatment
from white bus drivers. Furthermore, writes Stewart Burns,
she talked back to these abusive drivers, "ignored or defied
commands, reported drivers to the manager, or occasion-
ally engaged in physical self-defense. More and more often
[black women] refused to give up their seats to white people."[5] Periodically, like young Claudette Colvin, black

women not only refused to give their seats to whites but even resisted the police. Therefore, by the time Rosa Parks was arrested, black women's cup of endurance had fissured to the point of impossible repair. They needed a new cup.

The real initiative and leadership in the early stages of the Montgomery movement did not come from black ministers. Nor did it come from other black males in the city, although the trailblazing efforts of Vernon Johns were a significant exception. In addition, no black male—pastor or otherwise—agreed to be one of the plaintiffs in the suit that was filed in federal court challenging Alabama's segregation ordinance in public transportation. Only black women consented to be plaintiffs.

Generally the black ministers had to be pulled along by their church members. Jo Ann Robinson had this in mind when she said that church members were committed to supporting the boycott with or without their pastors. She claimed further that it was precisely because of this that the ministers then "decided that it was time for them, the leaders, to catch up with the masses."[6]

The discussion of the contributions of black women to the Montgomery struggle is significant. Many years passed before scholars, generally black women, began highlighting these contributions. Indeed, not only was it black women who proposed the boycott and who printed and distributed the leaflets announcing a one-day boycott, but they, more than black men, filled the churches during the numerous mass meetings that conveyed spiritual support to the protesters. We need also to remember that it was black women who, more often than black men, refused to vacate their seats for white bus passengers.

The Bus Boycott

After Rosa Parks was arrested, E. D. Nixon called local black pastors to drum up support for a one-day boycott. He called Ralph Abernathy first and got an immediate positive response. King was the third on his list and was, according to Nixon, the first to express apprehension. After calling fifteen other persons, Nixon again called King, who then agreed to participate. Having only been in Montgomery a little over a year, the twenty-six-year-old King felt it necessary to get to know the city and its leaders better. On one occasion he told Ralph Abernathy that this would likely take several years. Indeed, on reflection after the Supreme Court ruling that outlawed Alabama's segregation laws on November 13, 1956, King spoke of his initial apprehension about joining the protest:

> If anybody had asked me a year ago to head this movement, I tell you very honestly that I would

have run a mile to get away from it. I had no intention of being involved in this way. As I became involved, and as the people began to derive inspiration from their involvement, I realized that the choice leaves your own hands. The people expect you to give them leadership. You see them growing as they move into action, and then you know you no longer have a choice. You can't decide whether to stay in it or get out of it. You must stay in it.[7]

It might also be the case that in hesitating at first to get involved, King was also thinking about the invitation and

its implications. As a man of ideas, why would he not have needed a moment to ponder the matter, rather than give a spontaneous positive or negative response to Nixon's invitation?

When it seemed that the boycott had stalled, and several of the ministers asked if it would not be best to call it off, King—initially reluctant to get involved himself—reminded them who was really in charge. "If we went tonight and asked the people to get back on the bus, we would be ostracized," he said. "They wouldn't get back. . . . I believe to the bottom of my heart that the majority of Negroes would ostracize us. They are willing to walk."[8] King was convinced that the people themselves had had enough and were determined to surge forward, with or without their leaders. Some, like an elderly black woman, insisted that they were not marching for themselves but for their children and grandchildren.[9]

There were times when blacks exhibited signs of losing hope that the boycott would have a successful outcome. But their cup of endurance had run over, and they knew they could not turn back. Even black youth were determined. It was, after all, two young people—Claudette Colvin and Mary Louise Smith—who were plaintiffs in the federal lawsuit against Alabama's segregation ordinance. The case, *Browder v. Gayle*, was filed against Mayor W. A. Gayle and other Montgomery officials. Attorney Fred Gray and Martin Luther King tried unsuccessfully to get some black males, including black pastors, to step forward as plaintiffs in the federal lawsuit. Five black women stepped forward. Each had been subjected to humiliation on a city bus. One of the women, Jeannetta Reese, backed out, however. The other two (along with Colvin and Smith), Susie McDonald and Aurelia Browder, held firm. When

Colvin was asked in court, "Who was the leader of the boycott?" she answered, "Our leaders is just we ourself."[10]

On June 5, 1956, a panel of three federal judges ruled 2-1 that Montgomery and the state of Alabama's bus segregation statutes violated the fourteenth amendment. The greatest influencing factor was the landmark *Brown* decision two years earlier. The panel of federal judges suspended implementation of their decision pending the Supreme Court's ruling on the city's appeal. That ruling did not come until five months later, on November 13, 1956, while King and other leaders were on trial for operating a private enterprise (car pool) without a license. Although the ruling against legal segregation was only the beginning, it was a significant victory that helped launch King's civil and human rights ministry.

When the Supreme Court ruled against Alabama's state segregation law regarding public transportation, King and Abernathy boarded a bus and sat in the previously "whites only" section as reporters took pictures. Early that morning E. D. Nixon, Ralph Abernathy, Glenn Smiley, and Rosa Parks all arrived at King's home. Rosa Parks, however, the one whose arrest precipitated the boycott, was conspicuously absent on that first desegregated bus. When reporters asked later in the day if they could take pictures of her boarding buses downtown, she readily consented. The point here is that there was evidence of sexism early on in the movement, a topic to be taken up subsequently.

CHAPTER FIVE

Christian Love
and Gandhian Nonviolence

Martin Luther King's upbringing and education prepared him for leadership in the Montgomery bus boycott, and various faithful trailblazers prepared the black community for full participation, but closer inspection of the early months of the boycott reveal important developments in King's own ethical understanding. At the beginning of the boycott, King did not consciously apply Gandhian principles but depended almost solely on the love ethic of the Sermon on the Mount. In addition, he began the early days of the boycott as a staunch advocate of self-defense. He had armed guards around his house and kept a gun there for the protection of his family. We will see later what led to his ultimate rejection of these practices.

King often said that early on in Montgomery he and the protesters were more influenced by the unconditional love ethic of the Sermon on the Mount than anything else. "Christian love" and "the Sermon on the Mount," not "nonviolence" or any of the language associated with it, were the terms most often used. Terms such as "passive resistance," "nonviolent resistance," and "noncooperation" were used only after the protesters were more than two months into the boycott.

In the early days of the boycott, then, King essentially operated on the basis of what he knew best. He was a Christian minister who possessed a fundamentally sound understanding of the Bible and its basic principles. It was only natural that in the early stages of the campaign he appealed to biblical principles. We saw in chapter 2 that the spirit of nonviolence was prominent on the maternal side of King's family. But what prompted King to appeal to more explicitly Gandhian principles of nonviolence?

Influence of Bayard Rustin

Bayard Rustin, highly experienced in Gandhian principles and techniques, was urged by the Fellowship of Reconciliation (FOR) to go to Montgomery to advise King. When he arrived in late February 1956, two months after the boycott had begun, he discovered that King's was primarily an ethic of self-defense. King seemed comfortable having guns around his house and had simply not thought through the implications of this. Rather, he uncritically accepted the view that one was never to initiate violence but that one had a right to defend oneself and one's family.

Rustin was able to help King see the contradiction he was involved in as leader of a nonviolent protest movement. He recalled what he said to King:

> It was precisely what I discussed with Dr. King that, because the followers will seldom, in the mass, be dedicated to nonviolence in principle, that the leadership must be dedicated to it in principle, to keep those who believe in it as a tactic operating correctly. But if, in the flow and the heat of battle, a leader's house is bombed, and he shoots back, that is an encouragement to his followers to pick up guns. If, on the other hand, he has no guns around him, and they all know it, they will rise to the nonviolent occasion.[1]

King was much intrigued by this. Once he understood the necessity of leaders being absolutely devoted to nonviolence, he saw the contradiction in his teaching and practice and set out to rectify it.

King had no practical experience with Gandhian techniques and how best to implement them when he first met Rustin. Nor had he *thought* about basic ideas of nonviolence and what they must mean for one desiring to apply them in a noncooperation campaign. King began the boycott based on what he knew and was most comfortable with at the time—the teachings of the Sermon on the Mount.

Bayard Rustin had been a member of the Young Communist League, imprisoned for three years as a conscientious objector during World War II, and arrested on a charge of publicly engaging in a homosexual act in California two years before the boycott. Because of these things, some black leaders urged that he not be sent to Montgomery, since his background might prove detrimental to the movement.[2] His prior affiliation with the Communist Party and his arrest for a public homosexual act would be potentially devastating for the campaign if word got into the hands of white authorities in Montgomery. Significantly, there is no evidence that King was personally troubled about these aspects of Rustin's life.

Introduction to Gandhian Nonviolence

Mohandas K. Gandhi, India's supreme spiritual leader and nonviolent freedom fighter, was assassinated in January 1948 while King was a senior at Morehouse. It is likely that Benjamin Mays, who had a ninety-minute visit with Gandhi in 1936, at least mentioned this tragedy in one of his Tuesday chapel talks. If so, this was possibly the first time King heard Gandhi's name.

King was formally introduced to Gandhi's ethic of nonviolence in seminary. While there he heard well-known ecumenist and pacifist A. J. Muste lecture on pacifism, but

King was not converted to nonviolence. At the time he concluded that just because Gandhian principles worked in South Afrika and India this did not mean they would work in other countries. During his senior year he drove to the University of Pennsylvania in Philadelphia to hear Mordecai Johnson lecture on Gandhi. King reported that after the lectures he immediately went out and purchased about a half dozen books by and about Gandhi. It is not known how much of that literature he actually read at the time, but he was not then converted to Gandhian nonviolence. By 1958, however, King was described as "the Mahatma Gandhi in the present day American race crisis."[3]

King knew that the context of the Deep South was such that the Gandhian doctrine of nonviolence would have to undergo various adaptations in order to be relevant. Therefore, not every aspect of Gandhi's doctrine was adopted. For example, while he accepted Gandhi's insistence on the importance of undergoing a purification process that included longer and shorter periods of fasting prior to major nonviolent campaigns, he seldom fasted before demonstrations. Like Gandhi, King evolved from the idea of nonviolence as a mere strategy for social change to a firm conviction of nonviolence as a way of life. How did King's evolving ideas in this regard influence his practice? Conversely, how did his practice and experiments with Gandhian ideas and agape influence his emerging doctrine of nonviolence? To these questions we now turn.

Formal Elements of Nonviolence

As Martin Luther King began considering the merits of nonviolence during the bus boycott, like Gandhi he believed that his people had to muster the courage to carry out the experiment. He held that while Gandhi provided

the method for addressing social problems, Jesus Christ "furnished the spirit and motivation" through love. King's primary aim was not to win or to be successful, but to be faithful to the God who called him to ministry. Moreover, his sense of divine call was one of the key reasons he was able to persevere throughout his thirteen-year ministry.

King's ethic of nonviolence became a creative blending of Afrikan American, Christian, and Hindu elements that included (1) deep religious faith, (2) belief in the existence of an objective moral order and the conviction that the universe hinges on a moral foundation, (3) agape, (4) sin, (5) satyagraha, and (6) ahimsa. The latter two elements are the explicitly Hindu or Gandhian contributions.

For King, only a God who is fundamentally goodness and love could establish the world on a moral foundation.

If God is the source of goodness and love and established the universe on a moral foundation, it is reasonable to assert that things work best in the world when done nonviolently or without intentionally harming life in general and human life in particular. This was one of King's deepest convictions.

In some form all six concepts discussed below are included in Gandhi's concrete experiments with nonviolence. We will see that King brought something unique to the first four of these elements, quite possibly because he was Afrikan American and Christian and was reared in the Deep South. What follows is a brief discussion of the six elements of King's ethic of nonviolence.

Religious Faith

From the start of the Montgomery movement King incorporated the creative use of mass meetings, later strategically called prayer meetings. These meetings remained a central part of the practice of nonviolent protest demonstrations throughout his ministry. It was going to church to get spiritual food in preparation for the demonstrations that lay ahead. These prayer meetings, with King generally a featured speaker, probably did more to propel the protesters forward than any other single activity. Here they were reminded that they were not alone, and that God was with them every step of the way.

Generally the prayer meetings followed a basic pattern that was familiar to the vast majority of the protesters. There were "songs, prayer, Scripture reading, opening remarks by the president [King], collection, reports from various committees, and a 'pep talk.'"[4] The goal was to encourage, energize, and raise the level of expectation of the people for the day-to-day struggle. The songs, Scriptures, and prayers

85

were deliberately chosen to reinforce the emphasis on non-violence. Every speaker was asked to make nonviolence the central theme of his speech.

Every speech that King made at the prayer meetings revealed his increasing depth of understanding Gandhian nonviolence, how it worked, and what was required of every proponent. Reminiscent of Gandhi, he admonished the protesters that their aim must never be to defeat or humiliate white oppressors, but to win their respect and friendship.

Objective Moral Order and Moral Law

This principle is crucial for grounding theologically King's social ethics in general, and his ethics of nonviolence in particular. It suggests both that there is a reason to struggle against injustice and evil, and that the universe is structured in such a way that it provides companionship for those who take up the fight. Those who struggle against injustice, for example, need never feel that they are alone, or that God is not concerned about their well-being in the

world. In addition, this principle offers up the idea that the world works best when human beings endeavor to comply with moral law.

In the previous chapter we saw that as far back as his Morehouse College days King possessed a strong sense of the existence of an objective moral order and moral laws that govern the universe. Failure to comply with moral laws—the most significant of which is love—can have as detrimental and catastrophic consequences as the failure to comply with the physical laws of the universe. God "has placed within the very structure of this universe certain absolute moral laws," said King. "We can neither defy nor break them. If we disobey them, they will break us."[5]

Agape

King integrated the concept of agape (the spontaneous and overflowing love of God) into the theory of nonviolence in a way that gave it a more explicitly Christian tenor. But perhaps even more importantly, agape gave nonviolence a solid theological grounding. King understood God to be the source of agape. Indeed, following Swedish theologian Anders Nygren he held that God is agape, as well as the means by which love is instilled into the hearts and souls of human beings.[6] Nonviolence requires that one courageously confront and resist evil and injustice, but it also requires that it be done in the spirit of love.

The Kingian type of nonviolence requires love, but not a weak or sentimental kind. "It is a very stern love that would organize itself into collective action to right a wrong by taking on itself suffering," King wrote.[7] This is what makes Christianity so very difficult to live out, for as King observed during the Montgomery movement, "it demands a dangerous and costly altruism"—not just love of self but

love of neighbor.[8] For King, Christian agape was the highest good, "the most durable power," and the "heartbeat of the moral cosmos."[9]

Having been influenced by Paul Ramsey, King held that agape is disinterested love, which means that it expects nothing in return. It has no concern for who the neighbor is. *Everybody* is one's neighbor.

Under the influence of Nygren, King held that agape is the highest form of love and is "the most durable power in the world."[10] It is a love that is totally spontaneous and outpouring, whether its objects are the victims of the Virginia Tech tragedy on April 16, 2007, or the perpetrator in that tragedy, Tseung Qui Cho. According to King, every person is a recipient of God's agape—God's overflowing, inexhaustible love.

In addition, agape is redemptive love, the love of God working within human beings. Agape is directed even toward that which is deemed unlovable, and in reaching out to an object it actually imbues that object with value. The point of significance for King's doctrine of nonviolence is that agape *loves both because of and in spite of.* One can love one's enemies precisely because of God's agape (or the love of God in persons). Love in this sense is "the core and heartbeat of the cosmos."[11]

King was also convinced that agape is a thoroughly communal or relational principle. That is, persons are not created to exist in isolation. Instead, they are created in and for relationship and community. Agape always seeks to create, preserve, and enhance community.

Sin

King described sin as revolt against and separation or alienation from God, as an attempt to usurp God from the throne and to occupy it. Accordingly, "the gravest sin that one can committ [*sic*]" is "the sin of feeling [as the Pharisees did regarding the woman caught in adultery] that one has risen above the capacity for sin."[12] Sin, then, is humans' unwillingness and failure to accept their status as creatures. King believed with Reinhold Niebuhr that sin in its collective or group dimensions "rises to even more ominous proportions."[13] It is virtually impossible for the group, especially a nation, to see the mote in its own eye as easily and clearly as it sees the defects in others. King was certain that Christianity and the Bible are unmistakably clear that there are "tragic dimensions of the gonewrongness of human nature."[14] He therefore argued against the liberal notion that human beings are capable of reaching a sinless state.

King arrived at this realistic view of sin even before he entered seminary. What he needed—and what he received in seminary—was a formal theological framework to

support his understanding of sin. His study of Reinhold Niebuhr reminded him of the prevalence and obstinacy of sin. One sees the influence of Niebuhr in King's view that "sin is an ever present shower that sprinkles every one of us."[15] Sin therefore is present on every level of human achievement, and human beings are always in need of divine grace or mercy. But even with this there can be no assurance that human beings will ever overcome sin once for all.

Satyagraha

Satya means "truth," which is equivalent to love. In Hinduism, both truth and love are elements of the soul. *Agraha* means "firmness or force." *Satyagraha* therefore is "soul force," "love force," or "truth force." Unlike "passive resistance" or "nonresistance," it involves conscious, sustained action against evil or injustice. It requires that we "meet the forces of hate with the power of love; we must meet physical force with soul force," said King.[16] Nonviolence is "an extremely active force" and provides no room for cowardice and weakness. The proponent of nonviolence courageously confronts the opponent and does not run away. Like Gandhi, King preferred receiving violence to cowardice, declaring that "if cowardice is the only alternative to violence, it is better to fight."[17]

The effectiveness of satyagraha is not dependent upon the number of people involved in a nonviolent campaign, nor is it dependent upon the attitude and moral sense (or lack thereof) of the opponent. Rather, it depends upon the degree of commitment and firmness of the satyagrahi. If just a handful, even one person, commits to the true spirit of nonviolence as a way of life, the ultimate outcome of a civil rights demonstration can only be victorious.

Nonviolence is directed not against the opponent but against the evil or injustice. It is impossible to do this without devoting oneself to "a process of self-purification."[18] In "Letter from Birmingham Jail," King included self-purification as one of the four basic steps in nonviolent campaigns, although he did not say what this entailed. (The other three are fact gathering, negotiation, and direct action.) Rather than inflict suffering on the opponent, one invites and endures unearned suffering in support of a just cause. These are some of the redemptive qualities of satyagraha.

Ahimsa

This concept essentially focuses on human life. It literally means "noninjury." Under no circumstance should physical, emotional, or psychological harm be done to human beings. One who claims to practice ahimsa may fail in carrying out its requirements, but ahimsa as such does not fail. To understand the art of ahimsa is to know that it can do nothing but succeed, particularly in a world believed to hinge on a moral foundation.

Both King and Gandhi believed that human beings have been evolving toward ahimsa—and thus away from violence—at least from the time history began to be recorded. In part this is due to the increasing regard for persons as ends in themselves. King and Gandhi lived by the conviction that God is love and creates persons out of love and community for the purpose of living lovingly and justly in communal relations. In light of this, it must be that human beings will gradually come to the reality that what is required of them is

the noninjury of human beings. In this regard King said, "Man was born into barbarism when killing his fellow man was a normal condition of existence. He became endowed with a conscience. And he has now reached the day when violence toward another human being must become as abhorrent as eating another's flesh."[19]

Ahimsa means the noninjury and the nondestruction of life and thus points to the necessity of nonviolence. It is a comprehensive principle that is grounded in the idea of the unity and goodness of all life. King came to this idea of the interrelatedness of all life as a result of the values instilled in him as a child. The theological and moral significance of the idea is that everything that is done affects every person, including the divine Person, either directly or indirectly. The logic of the concept of the unity of all life is that a violent counterattack on the opponent is also an attack on oneself and on God. King agreed with Gandhi's affirmation that "we are all tarred with the same brush, and are children of one and the same Creator."[20]

Like Gandhi, King held that nonviolence must avoid not only physical violence "but internal violence of spirit."[21] The devotee of nonviolence not only refuses to do physical harm to an opponent. She also refuses to hate or otherwise think ill of the opponent or to call her names. For King, the rationale behind this was simple: "At the center of nonviolence stands the principle of love. The nonviolent resister would contend that in the struggle for human dignity, the oppressed people of the world must not succumb to the temptation of becoming bitter or indulging in hate campaigns. To retaliate in kind would do nothing but intensify the existence of hate in the universe."[22] The concepts discussed in this section converge and are interrelated in the full-blown nonviolence of King—that is, nonviolence as a creed or a way of relating and being in the world.

Training in Nonviolence

King received instructions and training from Bayard Rustin and Glenn Smiley on how to lead nonviolent training sessions. The first of these occurred at one of the prayer meetings in early October 1956, ten months into the boycott. Using the technique of "socio-drama" (a method later popularized during the sit-ins and freedom rides), King asked for two volunteers to stand and state—for all to hear—how they planned to behave once they returned to the buses and in the event they sat next to a white person who was hostile and insulting toward them, even to the point of shoving them. The first volunteer said that she would be upset at such treatment but that she would not move. Her inclination would be to ignore the person and just let others observe his or her ignorant behavior. However, were she shoved she said she might be inclined to respond in kind. King thanked her for her honest response and then proceeded to ask her what would be achieved by shoving the person. The woman agreed when the audience said that nothing would be gained.

The other volunteer was more philosophical, remarking that it was important for them to remember that whites do not know blacks as well as blacks know them. "It isn't going to do any good to get mad and strike back, 'cause that's just what some of them *want* us to do." She said that blacks fought too long and hard to desegregate the buses, and it was important for them to behave with dignity and act "like good Christian ladies and gentlemen."[23] After this, King informed the group that there would be many more sessions like this. On December 3–9, 1956, the Montgomery Improvement Association (MIA) held its first Annual Institute on Nonviolence and Social Change, which featured seminars on theory and training for implementing nonviolence, voter registration, and education.

There was nothing formal about these early training sessions on nonviolence. By the Birmingham campaign in 1963, however, the process was much more sophisticated. It included lots of role-playing or socio-drama, with one or more parties simulating the behavior of white supremacists and others simulating the appropriate and acceptable nonviolent response. In addition, by this time demonstrators had to sign pledge cards indicating that they would adhere to nonviolent principles during the demonstrations. One was not turned away merely because she could not do this, but she was not allowed to demonstrate. Those who did not believe they could retain their composure in the ranks of the demonstrators were invited to answer telephones, type, file, run errands, and perform other tasks.

CHAPTER SIX

The Power and Persuasion of Youth

There is seldom discussion of King's utter love, adoration, and respect for children. Pictures of Vietnamese children severely or mortally wounded by napalm bombs broke his heart and contributed to his decision to break silence on the Vietnam War in 1967. King envisioned a world in which children and youth would have all of the things that are necessary for a life that is truly worth living. More so, he believed that they could make constructive contributions toward achieving freedom and liberation and that strategically there could be times when children and youth could energize a freedom campaign, as they did in the Birmingham movement in 1963. Indeed, it was black youth who sparked the sit-ins in 1960 and continued the stalled freedom rides in 1961.

Without question King respected the dignity and worth of children as human beings.[1] He felt a real sense of commitment to their well-being. Indeed, there were even times when King appeared to be lonely for children. So frequently away from home in the struggle for freedom, he missed his own children in the worst way. It should come as no surprise that he was so open, gentle, and patient with children in Birmingham, Selma, and other cities. In a way, many of these were King's surrogate children—his children away from home. In a fatherly sort of way he could be very protective of the children he encountered in the various movement campaigns.

In virtually every campaign, from Montgomery to Memphis, youth were involved. Although Afrikan American youth in Montgomery did not ride the buses to school and other places during the boycott, there were no explicit plans for how they were to be utilized in a strategic way, such as occurred during the Birmingham campaign eight years later. And yet Montgomery black youth were much involved in and committed to the boycott. King came to understand that young people were, like their parents and other adults, self-determining beings who could decide for themselves how to respond to the injustice that they too experienced each day. A consideration of recollections of some adults regarding the role they played when they were young people during the early movement years follows.[2]

Montgomery

When Martin Luther King assumed full-time pastoral responsibilities at Dexter Avenue Baptist Church, his aim was to put the ministry on a solid footing while also getting to know the city and its leaders in all areas. Because of his interest in religion and social problems, he established the Social and Political Action Committee. The committee had a twofold responsibility: to keep before the congregation the importance of the NAACP and membership in it, and also to hold forums to discuss and address social problems adversely affecting blacks in Montgomery. From this we can see that at the outset King laid a strong foundation for social gospel ministry.

King knew that Rosa Parks was not the first black woman to be arrested for not giving her bus seat to a white person. He was in fact part of the ad hoc committee that met with the police commissioner about the earlier arrest of Claudette Colvin. King also knew about Mary Louise Smith's arrest.

Colvin's resistance to being removed from the bus exhibited what all of the young people who were involved in the movement were willing to do. They had a real stake in what was happening in their city, especially when they were being hurt and otherwise demeaned by the policies and practices of white racists. Therefore, many black youth decided that if they were old enough to recognize that they were being treated inhumanely, they were old enough to resist.

The black woman history teacher who taught Colvin and her classmates about the Constitution and about their

Afrikan heritage made a lasting impression on her. She developed almost overnight a new sense of pride and dignity. Colvin said that her teacher "really had pricked my mind, so I went home and I washed my hair and I didn't straighten it."[3]

Looking back on the Montgomery experience after forty years, Colvin told Ellen Levine that she had grown up in that city and was taught by her parents that blacks had their place and whites had theirs. She also recalled being able to buy things at the downtown department stores but not being allowed to eat food at the lunch counter: "You could buy, but you couldn't sit down and eat there. When I realized that, I was really angry."[4] Furthermore, certain stores would not allow blacks to try on clothing items. Colvin and other young people rebelled against such practices.

Not surprisingly, Colvin and her friends concluded that "the older [black] people let white people get away with it. They never said they didn't like it. Older black people were always respectful to white people. But the younger blacks began to rebel."[5] She recalled that black youth were angered the most when a classmate, Jeremiah Reeves, was accused of assaulting and raping a white woman. Reeves consistently denied even having consensual sex with the woman. The NAACP hired lawyers to defend him, but lost the case. Reeves was kept in jail until he was of age, and then he was electrocuted in 1958. Reeves was sentenced about two years before King's arrival in Montgomery, but he heard about it, and in 1958 he led a group of fifteen black ministers in a procession to the statehouse to protest the execution.

Joseph Lacey was a thirteen-year-old when the bus boycott began. He remembered how excited he and other black youth were as they anticipated the first day of the boycott. They were even more excited walking to school and being passed by empty buses: "It was just a beautiful thing. It was a day to behold to see nobody on the bus." There was much camaraderie and togetherness among black youth and adults, he recalled. They all "walked and enjoyed walking," because they were walking for their freedom and the freedom of those who would follow them. "Everybody felt like a part of the struggle because everybody had a part."[6] Lacey believed that even some whites boycotted the buses as a sign of sympathy with the cause.

Black parents were concerned both about the safety of their children and retaining their jobs. However, many

young people, such as Fred Taylor, wanted their teachers to discuss with them what was happening in Montgomery during the boycott. Taylor and others secretly attended the mass meetings against their parents' instructions. Like many young people, he remembered how King's declaration at the prayer meetings that black people are somebody began to change his impression of himself and his outlook on his family. "It was right during the boycott that I began to have a different assessment of myself as an individual and to feel my sense of worth."[7]

When the Supreme Court pronounced Alabama's segregation ordinance to be unconstitutional in November 1956, Taylor and other youth followed the instructions of the leaders on how to groom and dress when they returned to the buses. Taylor sat proudly behind the bus driver. He would sit next to a white man but not a white woman. For him, as for many black youth, the Jeremiah Reeves incident still rubbed raw nerves. This meant, in part, that even though the Court had outlawed the segregation ordinance, whites and blacks in Montgomery were far from being a real community. Nevertheless, the Montgomery campaign did much to inspire the passing of the Civil Rights Acts of 1957 and 1960.

The remainder of the 1950s after the boycott was a time of organizing and experimenting with means of enhancing the movement. King sought ways both to continue and expand the movement throughout the South. In February 1957, what came to be the Southern Christian Leadership Conference (SCLC) was formed for this purpose. Its motto was "to save the soul of America." King published his first book, *Stride toward Freedom: The Montgomery Story* in 1958. He went to India, the land of Gandhi, in 1959 to learn what he could about Gandhi's method and how it might be adapted.

As it became increasingly clear that he could not stay abreast of his pastoral duties at Dexter and tend to the fledgling SCLC, King resigned in November 1959 and became a copastor of Ebenezer Baptist Church in Atlanta, where his father was senior minister. Approximately three months later, on February 1, 1960, four black freshmen males at Greensboro Agricultural and Technical College in North Carolina sat at a "whites only" lunch counter in Woolworth's, asked to be served, and refused to leave when service was denied. With this, the sit-in direct action movement began. Within two months students—black and white—were sitting-in in more than fifty cities in nine states. By this time, Woolworth's had lost so much revenue that executives quietly desegregated its lunch counters. It is most significant that the initial sit-in was initiated by black youth, thus effectively removing exclusive control of

the movement from their elders. Although King had relatively little to do with the sit-ins and the freedom rides (which began on May 4, 1961), the media and others erroneously cast him in the role of their mastermind and leader.

Nevertheless, King applauded and supported the sit-ins and the Student Nonviolent Coordinating Committee (SNCC), which was a direct result of this action tactic. King's next opportunity to lead a civil rights campaign came in 1961 when some local leaders in Albany, Georgia, invited him and the SCLC to join their struggle for civil rights. By all accounts, including King's, the Albany movement was a failure. However, the movement's efforts continued to bubble up across the South in the next few years.

Birmingham

So many black churches and homes had been bombed by white racists by the early 1960s that Birmingham, Alabama, was given the nickname "Bombingham." One black neighborhood was bombed so frequently that it was known as "Dynamite Hill." King described Birmingham as the most segregated city in America. Like most major cities in the South, its leaders defied all efforts toward desegregation. The racism in Birmingham during that period was often blatant, vicious, and deadly. Police Commissioner Eugene "Bull" Connor brought all resources to bear on upholding the state's segregation code.

Long before Birmingham became a part of the formal civil rights movement in 1963, Reverend Fred Shuttlesworth, pastor of Bethel Baptist Church, organized and led numerous civil rights demonstrations during the 1950s, concurrent with the Montgomery bus boycott. He also preached and spoke at mass meetings and was a member of the MIA. Although he got only minimal participation from

Birmingham's black citizens, he remained fearless and undaunted. Shuttlesworth founded the Alabama Christian Movement for Human Rights (ACMHR) after state authorities banned the NAACP in 1956. The goal of the ACMHR was to press for desegregation of all city facilities. The response of white segregationists was brutal. Shuttlesworth was beaten several times, his house was bombed on Christmas day in 1956, and his church was bombed multiple times. Bull Connor and his white supremacist henchmen were implicated in the church bombings but were never prosecuted.

Although black youth, including Shuttlesworth's children, Ricky, Pat, and Fred Jr., were avid participants in the pre-SCLC civil rights campaign in Birmingham, I focus here on their involvement in the movement *after* Shuttlesworth successfully lobbied King and the SCLC to come to town. King committed to this in January 1963. The campaign was named Project C (Confrontation). It was launched on April 3 with Miles College students staging sit-ins at five downtown department stores. From then on there were marches to city hall and meetings with black community leaders, including businessmen and pastors, to enlist support. This was difficult work, since black leaders and pastors considered King and the SCLC to be outsiders coming in to stir up things, which they believed would only make life more difficult for them. King finally convinced many of them that "no Negro, in fact no American, is an outsider when he goes to any community to aid in the cause of freedom and justice."[8]

When King decided to violate a temporary injunction against demonstrations, fourteen-year-old Bernita Roberson chose to disobey her father and to march with King. She and many other youths were arrested along with him. At the county jail the children were removed to the juvenile holding area. Roberson recalled that King hugged each of the children and shook their hands as they walked by. Each of the youth felt good and reassured because they believed they had made a difference. The next day, eight white clergymen published an open letter to King, calling his demonstrations "unwise" and "untimely." This prompted King's famous "Letter from Birmingham Jail," a literary and theological classic.

In the letter, King provides his theological and ethical rationale for being in Birmingham and generally affirms that *every* Christian is called and obligated to act for justice on the basis of the love ethic of Christianity. Because of the interrelated structure of reality, King said that justice is indivisible. He told the white clergymen, "Injustice anywhere is a threat to justice everywhere. We are caught in an inescapable network of mutuality, tied in a single garment of destiny. Whatever affects one directly, affects all indirectly."[9]

In addition to explaining the steps involved in noncooperation campaigns, the letter distinguished between just and unjust laws and what is required of one who confronts an unjust law. It also expressed King's deep disappointment in the white moderates who were more concerned about law and order than justice. The letter also expressed King's dismay that the white church and its leaders failed to be voices for justice.

From the beginning King believed students' involvement would be needed if the campaign were to succeed.[10] By the middle of April 1963 the Birmingham campaign had stalled, and defeat seemed inevitable. King sent for James Bevel, who at the time was working on voter registration in Mississippi.

When King met with the passionate Bevel and the rest of the SCLC staff, Bevel proposed that they use schoolchildren in the marches. The jails were already filled with

black adults, and there were few left to carry on the mass demonstrations. However, there were vast numbers of children. Moreover, Bevel argued, black children in the Deep South considered themselves "at least partially free,"[11] unlike many black adults. This was a lesson he and his wife, Diane Nash Bevel, learned during their work in Mississippi. Experience told him that it was black youth, more than their parents and other adults, who were willing and courageous enough to take real risks for freedom.

From that point the Birmingham campaign became *a children's crusade for freedom*. When some of the first children were arrested for violating the injunction against demonstrations and transported to the county jail, King talked with them outside the fenced area. This eased their anxiety.

On reflection King spoke favorably of having included the children. "But most of all," he said, "we were inspired with a desire to give to our young a true sense of their own stake in freedom and justice. We believed they would have the courage to respond to our call."[12] In addition, King was convinced that introducing the children into the campaign "was one of the wisest moves we made. It brought a new impact to the crusade, and the impetus we needed to win the struggle."[13] He reported that when an eight-year-old marcher was asked by an amused police officer what she wanted, she eyeballed him and said, "F'eedom." The children brought energy and hope to the stalled campaign and were the reason their parents and other black adults got behind the movement.[14] James Bevel had convinced the young people that it was up to them to free their parents, teachers, themselves, and the country.[15]

Without question the massive hordes of students—ranging from third grade to college—caught Birmingham authorities completely off guard. Wave after wave of students left various church locations to march downtown. They quickly filled all available paddy wagons. Bull Connor had to use police cars and school buses to transport the growing numbers of youth to jail. When there was no jail space left the children were transported to the state fairgrounds as a temporary prison. David Halberstam reflects that it was estimated that by the time the children's crusade ended, approximately ten thousand children had been jailed in Birmingham.[16] In some instances third-graders were in jail as long as a full week.

When Bull Connor ordered his men to use high-powered water hoses and attack dogs on the marching children, it was all captured on national television. This brutal treatment of innocent children who were demonstrating for the right to be treated like human beings was not received well by many around the country and around the world who were at the dinner table when the pictures were flashed over television news. Halberstam notes that "Birmingham became, to the rest of the nation, not so much a city but an image, and a devastating one at that, where white cops could use maximum force on children trying to exercise constitutional rights."[17]

The abuse of black children as seen on national television backfired on Birmingham authorities and forced their hand. This led them to work out an acceptable agreement with King and the SCLC that included desegregating downtown stores and hiring black clerks and salespersons. The day after the agreement rabid segregationists bombed the home of King's brother and also planted a bomb near the Gaston Motel, where King was staying, but he was not in the motel when the bomb detonated.

Tragically, that same year, after the March on Washington to end discrimination and violence against blacks, the Sixteenth Street Baptist Church in Birmingham was bombed on September 15, 1963, killing four black girls in their early teens. Addie Mae Collins, Denise McNair, Cynthia Wesley, and Carole Robertson had been in Sunday school. King eulogized Collins, Wesley, and McNair, whose funerals were held together, as "the martyred heroines of a holy crusade for freedom and human dignity."[18] King expressed further his love and hope for children in general when he said that babies are "the latest news from heaven" and children "are a glorious promise."[19]

Mississippi Delta

By 1961 the movement was focusing on multiple fronts at once. Sit-ins and freedom rides sought to desegregate lunch counters and interstate transportation throughout the South. The ideas from his home upbringing and his formal education continued to inform King's energetic leadership.

The state of Alabama, particularly Birmingham and Selma, were frightening places for blacks, but the Mississippi Delta region was in a category all its own in this regard. Most blacks and liberal whites rightly suspected that the Klan and White Citizens Councils were thoroughly embedded in the political, legal, judicial, and educational systems of that region. This explains in part how officials in Mississippi were able, with impunity, to become so proficient at making blacks disappear from jails, their homes, or right off the street. Every black and white person who did civil rights work in Mississippi knew how quickly and easily this could happen. This is why SNCC had a rule in Mississippi that workers were never to violate under any circumstances: *No one was to ride alone, whether in a car or on a bus.*[20] Roy DeBerry was in high school in the early 1960s in Holly Springs, Mississippi. He recalled that anybody who was a part of the movement "knew that when you disappear in Mississippi, you're dead."[21]

In virtually any place in the South, King's presence generated in blacks a sense of excitement and hope. Generally the meeting place would be filled to capacity and overflowing. But this was not the case in 1961 when James Lawson was in Jackson, Mississippi, with King doing a workshop on nonviolence. According to Halberstam, Lawson recalled that the meeting place for the workshop was only half-filled and those present were clearly uneasy about

being there. "A King audience was usually a confident one and more often than not an exuberant one, but not in this case."[22] The atmosphere was thick with anxiety, as attendees quite accurately assumed they were under surveillance and that their names might be released to the white supremacist authorities. Mississippi was known even by movement people to be the state they would have to crack if the movement in general was to have a chance to succeed. But the cost could be deadly—and was.

When Bernard Lafayette and two other students, James Bevel and John Lewis, boarded a bus in 1961 with C. T. Vivian and James Lawson in Montgomery, Alabama, for a freedom ride to Jackson, Mississippi, the image that came to Lafayette's mind about black people in Mississippi was of them hanging from trees with ropes around their necks. Mississippi, particularly the Delta and Southwest regions of the state, was not friendly to black people. Blacks literally had no political rights in the state, nor could they count on the police and the judicial system for protection.

The young blacks of SNCC led the way in the Mississippi Delta campaign. It was they who inspired Ruleville, Mississippi, native Fannie Lou Hamer to join the voter registration campaign, thus launching her as a grassroots leader. The presence of SNCC youth in the Delta was the beginning of what would soon include hundreds of Northern white college students from all over the country working with local black activists in a massive voter registration campaign in the most violent state in the country. About a year later other civil rights organizations such as CORE, NAACP, and SCLC joined SNCC to form the Council of Federated Organizations (COFO), and together they began planning for a massive voter registration drive in the state. To this end they planned "Freedom Summer" for 1964. The aim was to bring more than a thousand students, mostly white, to the state to work on the campaign. King described this effort as "one of the most creative attempts I had seen to radically change the oppressive life of the Negro in that entire state and possibly the entire nation."[23]

Tragedy struck before the young people could make much headway. At the beginning of the summer Michael Schwerner, Andrew Goodman (both white Northerners and Jewish), and James Chaney (a black Mississippian) went to Philadelphia, Mississippi, to investigate the burning of a black church. They drove there on a Sunday morning, June 21, 1964, and disappeared. Their mutilated bodies were found on August 4. While searching for the three youth, authorities found the bodies of seven other blacks who had disappeared.

As King was making plans to go to Mississippi again to assist in the civil rights effort he received word that a white supremacist guerrilla group was plotting to assassinate him

when he arrived. He rejected advice to cancel the trip, saying, "If I were constantly worried about death, I could not function."[24] Always aware of his call to ministry and the fact that he was much in the national spotlight, the thirty-four-year-old King concluded that he simply had to come to terms with the possibility that his life could be taken at any moment.

King arrived in Mississippi one month after the disappearance of the three civil rights activists. Tragically and ironically, the murders occurred not long after the passage of the Civil Rights Act of 1964. King had nothing but praise for the work of the SNCC youth and the young white college students who descended on the state during Freedom Summer. He spent time touring a number of the poorest areas of the Delta, meeting and talking with impoverished blacks, many of whom lived in shacks with dirt floors.

The young people most assuredly—and realistically—held some fear of Mississippi. Yet their commitment to working for justice would not allow them to avoid bringing the movement to that most intimidating state. They knew that their involvement could prove deadly for some of their number and also for local residents who were brave enough to work with them. Yet these young people pressed forward.

Selma

Selma was Alabama's most rabidly racist area. The majority of whites expected blacks to remain submissive. Because whites were so vicious and blacks so passive and fearful, SNCC worker Bernard Lafayette, veteran of the 1961 freedom ride to Jackson, Mississippi, accepted the leadership of the Selma project, although friends strongly urged him not to. SNCC had received information that the Justice Department would be going to Selma to examine its voter registration practices. It had evidence that Selma was the textbook example—in the so-called Black Belt areas of the South—of fraudulently denying blacks the right to register and vote. Fifteen thousand blacks were eligible to vote in Selma. Less than 1 percent were registered.

Lafayette knew that if SNCC could make a significant inroad into Selma, this would go a long way toward pressuring the federal government to work on a voting rights bill. When Lafayette went to Selma in 1962 to scout the place, the whites seemed meaner and angrier than other white Alabamans, while the blacks were nervous and suspicious of him and avoided him. In addition, local black ministers literally preached against him, telling parishioners that he was an outside agitator who had come to make trouble for them.

Many said that the sheriff, Jim Clark, was more vicious than Bull Conner. King referred to Clark with his "Gestapo-like control" as one of the main roadblocks in

Selma. There was, said King, "a carefully cultivated mystique behind the power and brutality" of men like Jim Clark. "The gun, the club, and the cattle prod produced the fear that was the main barrier to voting."[25] Ironically, Clark's mean-spiritedness toward blacks backfired when he and his men stormed into the memorial service of a much admired black man with a court order claiming that they had a right to be there to ensure that no laws were being broken. In addition, Clark took pictures of blacks entering the church. Mourners were outraged by this breach of respect and began to rally, feeling that they could overcome their own historic fear and unite in the struggle. King was convinced that if blacks in Selma had the vote, "there would be no Jim Clarks, there would be no oppressive poverty directed against Negroes."[26]

Like the voter registration work in the Mississippi Delta, the work in Selma was started by SNCC youth. By the time King and the SCLC entered Selma in January 1965, Lafayette and SNCC had already done substantial groundbreaking work. Because of the work and sacrifices of black youth, the elders were able to hit the ground running.

It is of interest that Bernard Lafayette and other SNCC youth such as James Bevel, Diane Nash, Bob Moses, and John Lewis had already figured out from their early work in Mississippi that passage of a civil rights bill—important as that would be—would not be sufficient if blacks in the South did not also have the right to register, vote, and have their vote count. This was an example of the youth being more in touch with the pulse of what needed to happen than some of the older leadership in the SCLC and other civil rights organizations. Like the SNCC youth, King too had a strong sense before 1965 that the passage of a civil rights bill would not be sufficient to guarantee that Southern blacks could vote.[27]

King's Love and Respect for the Children

Martin Luther King knew that every Afrikan American—indeed every American—regardless of gender, class, and age, was adversely affected by racism. King believed that children who had a sense of being unjustly treated because of their race had every right to participate in organized efforts to protest such treatment. They were no less sacred before God than adults.

King knew in advance that he would be scathingly criticized by black parents and others for putting the children in harm's way in Birmingham. Indeed, for his involving children he was harshly criticized by black Birmingham businessman A. G. Gaston, as well as by Malcolm X and Thurgood Marshall. Intellectually and even strategically, King was convinced that involving the children on the front line in the movement was the right thing to do. Many children took it upon themselves to participate in demonstrations even in defiance of their parents and school officials. Such behavior only confirmed for King that children not only had a major stake in the struggle against racial injustice but also had a strong awareness of what was going on. They *wanted* to participate and would do so in defiance of any adults.

One more example may help demonstrate the accuracy of King's belief. Sheyann Webb was a resident of the George Washington Carver housing projects in Selma when King arrived. As an eight-year-old, she was walking to school one day when she saw a large number of blacks and whites talking together at the Brown Chapel AME Church, the place where mass meetings were held. To this eight-year-old, the mingling of blacks and whites together seemed quite unusual in light of what she had grown accustomed to seeing in Selma. Out of curiosity, she went over to the crowd and followed them into the church. Once there she heard Hosea Williams speaking about voter registration from the pulpit. She remembered him talking about Martin Luther King.

Sheyann Webb participated in the infamous "Bloody Sunday" march on the Pettus Bridge in Selma on March 7, 1965. Afterward her parents, as well as many teachers, began attending the mass meetings. Webb also participated in the march from Selma to Montgomery that began on

March 21. When King saw Webb standing alone, he inquired as to who she was with. Upon learning that she was alone, he placed her in the care of his staff and instructed them to contact her parents. This was more than a gesture on the part of King. His action was one of genuine concern for the well-being of a young child who was without parental supervision and who was fighting for her freedom.

CHAPTER SEVEN

Against Racism, Economic Exploitation, and War

By the time Martin Luther King received the Nobel Peace Prize on December 10, 1964, he was well on the way to developing a universal human rights outlook. The civil rights campaigns in Montgomery, Birmingham, the Mississippi Delta, Selma, and other places in the Deep South, coupled with his theological conviction that persons are created by the one God of the universe and thus are interdependent, had already convinced King that God is concerned not merely about the rights of and justice for blacks, but for all people—nationally and internationally. He had already developed a strong sense of the need to emphasize *human* rights and justice for all people. This did not mean that King intended to reduce his emphasis on civil rights and racism, only that he needed to expand his moral outlook to include the enhancement of the humanity, rights, and dignity of all people.

This pattern of expanding his moral outlook and including more social issues was in line with King's adherence to the Hegelian dictum that "the truth is the whole." By the mid-1960s King knew that blacks were not just victims of racism but that something about racism also made them more vulnerable to poverty and other forms of economic exploitation. This in turn seemed to make blacks and other poor people, including whites, the most susceptible to being sent to Vietnam and other war zones to essentially fight wars against innocent people of color in order to protect the economic interests of wealthy citizens of the United States of America. These three social problems—racism, poverty, and war—were not just separate isolated issues for Martin Luther King. More and more he saw them as part of a whole, such that to effectively address any one of them, all had to be addressed.

Therefore it is not correct to say that whereas King began his civil rights ministry by focusing solely on racism, he later put this behind him and began to focus on issues such as poverty, peace, and war. Rather, as his thinking evolved and his level of awareness increased, his moral field expanded to include other important social issues. When King was accused of spending too much time on peace issues rather than civil rights in the late 1960s, he responded, "I don't spend that much time on the peace question or on Vietnam. Because ninety-five percent of my time is still spent in the civil rights struggle."[1] Four days before he was assassinated, King said that one of the remaining great challenges to this country is to rid itself of the last vestiges of racism, for it is "still the black man's burden and the white man's shame"; it is still "a way of life for the vast majority of white Americans."[2] King put the matter simply: "The roots of racism are very deep in our country."[3] In other words, King insisted right up to the

end that racism was endemic to American institutions and threatened to poison "a whole body politic" if all forms of it were not eradicated.[4]

From the time he entered seminary, Martin Luther King was committed to addressing and eliminating a trilogy of interconnected social problems: racism, militarism, poverty and economic injustice. He vowed to never adjust to these social evils. In a number of his last speeches, sermons, writings, and interviews King challenged this nation to do four things if it hoped to live as God expects nations to live: (1) to develop an internationalist human rights, or "world house," perspective, (2) to rid itself of the last vestiges of racism, (3) to address the issue of massive poverty, and (4) to acknowledge its militarism, eliminate it, and internationalize nonviolence. This chapter will discuss these and related challenges, as well as some of the basic theological and philosophical foundations on which King grounded them.

World House Perspective

In a paper written during his senior year in seminary, King wrote that "the gist of the world's problem really is: a lack of world brotherhood" and that there is a need to "rise from the narrow horizon of clashing nationalism to the wide horizon of world cooperation."[5] By this time he had taken a number of courses in Bible and had also been formally introduced to the philosophy of personalism. Together these confirmed for King his conviction about the interrelated structure of reality and the need for a world house perspective.

King held that there is one God of the universe who is creator and sustainer of all things, who created human beings as members of one family under God and imbued all with the divine image of God. Persons are so thoroughly interrelated in this sense that what affects one—any place in the world—affects all others, including God, directly or indirectly. This is a basic claim of Christianity, as well as personalism. From this King reasoned that while it is reasonable for one to be concerned about the well-being of one's own group or nation, it is unreasonable and theologically inappropriate to focus exclusively on one's group while failing to recognize its mutual relationship to other groups. King therefore rejected exclusivist or chauvinistic forms of nationalism.

Christian personalism required a human rights, or "world house," perspective. This did not mean that the

various individual groups (e.g., Afrikan Americans) should not continue to struggle against injustices perpetrated against them. It did mean, however, that they should not be blind to their membership in the larger world house— that God created humans as many, to live as one under God. All groups, King held, must understand this basic interrelatedness with others in the world house.

As important as equality is between whites and blacks, King said, it "will not solve the problems of either . . . if it means equality in a world society stricken by poverty and in a universe doomed to extinction by war."[6] Each group rightly focuses on issues specific to itself and its own room so to speak, while also striving to be aware of major issues affecting other parts of the house. The latter has implications for the well-being of every other group. There is nothing wrong with group loyalty unless it is rigid and chauvinistic. King's theology called for an *ecumenical* loyalty: "Every nation must now develop an overriding loyalty to mankind as a whole in order to preserve the best in their individual societies."[7]

The Christian personalist conviction that God creates persons to be in relationship, to live in a special type of community (what King called the beloved community), means that while every individual has a basic individuality and autonomy, what each does affects and is affected by others. It means that no individual, group, or nation can be all that they can be in isolation. There is a fundamental unity about the world and the people in it, such that "anyone who feels that he can live alone is sleeping through a revolution," King said. This is especially the case today with the almost daily lightening speed advancements in the use of the Internet. To a large extent the computer, more than any other single scientific or technological advancement, has only confirmed (in a technological sense) what science, philosophy, and theology have posited for many years—namely, that the world is essentially one. King applauded this idea but just as quickly charged that the real challenge is for human beings "to make the world one in terms of brotherhood."[8] Unfortunately, the United States and other nations have lacked the moral resolve to do this.

For King, advances in science far outdistanced those in the areas of morality and community making. This will continue to be a challenge as long as human beings fail to understand that God has structured reality in such a way that all persons are interrelated and interdependent. It is not just a matter of self-survival, but of being concerned about the survival of others as well.

Eradicate All Vestiges of Racism

King knew early on that the church, "the moral guardian" and conscience of the state, nation, and world was the greatest purveyor of racism. In seminary he argued that "the church is suppose [*sic*] to be the most radical opposer of the status quo in society, yet, in many instances, it is the greatest preserver of the status quo."[9] Enslavement of Afrikans in this country received the sanction of the church. The lynching of blacks prior to, during, and after Reconstruction was frequently done by whites who boasted of attending church on a regular basis to worship Jesus Christ. From the beginning to the end of his ministry, King believed that "the church is one of the chief exponents of racial bigotry" and racism "is America's greatest moral dilemma."[10]

We have seen that King appreciated orthodox Christianity's recognition of sin. However, he was critical of its tendency to focus on "sins of the flesh" such as excessive

drinking, profanity, stealing, and fornication, while remaining almost completely silent on sins such as racism, militarism, and poverty that have devastating and often deadly consequences for vast numbers of people. King wanted the church to focus more on these types of sins. He lamented the fact that for many white Christians it was deemed unchristian to drink or gamble, but not to enslave a people against its will and to subject them to ongoing racial discrimination.[11]

By 1967 Martin Luther King remained adamant that "racism is still that hound of hell which dogs the tracks of our civilization."[12] He saw white racism as "the chief destructive cutting edge" that was splitting the nation into two hostile societies.[13] Moreover, racism was not just an American phenomenon but a world phenomenon. Even today we see the residue of racism from European and

130

American colonial rule in Afrika, Asia, and Latin America. In the United States we see more than its residue.

For there to be the slightest hope that the world house will be transformed into a beloved community, it is necessary to be vigilant in efforts to eradicate all vestiges of racism in every area of society. If, as King maintains, God is "the Father of all" persons, then racism is a sin against God and all of humanity, since it is based on the alienation of one race from another and thus from God. King's Christian personalism convinced him that *every* person is infinitely precious to God. This being the case, racism has no place in a world house or internationalist perspective.

Rid the Nation and World of Poverty

Five months before the Montgomery bus boycott, in an address that sounds surprisingly contemporary, King spelled out the economic problems that were adversely affecting large numbers of blacks and other Americans: "In every community people are hungry, unemployment is rising like a tidal wave, housing conditions are embarrassingly poor, crime and juvenile [*sic*] delinquency are spreading like the dew drops on an early fall morning. All of these conditions result from the economic problem."[14] Until these and related issues are addressed and eradicated there will be little significant advancement toward the beloved community. Creative living in the world house will also be questionable.

For King, too many people all over the world lived in horrendously impoverished conditions: "Two-thirds of the peoples of the world go to bed hungry at night. They are undernourished, ill-housed and shabbily clad. Many of them have no houses or beds to sleep in. Their only beds are the sidewalks of the cities and the dusty roads of the villages."[15]

King saw this crushing poverty in the United States (the ghettos of the North, the rural areas of the South, and Appalachia), India, Afrika, and Latin America. Because of his belief in the interrelated structure of reality, he was certain that the destiny of the poor in each of these places was inextricably linked with that of the others. As King witnessed the heart-wrenching poverty in the United States and other nations of the world, he recalled that a large chunk of the U.S. budget was devoted to paying for military bases around the world that acted to protect the interests of the wealthy. In addition, he resented the fact that the federal government was spending tens of millions of dollars to store surplus food. The better storage places, he contended, are the empty stomachs of poor people all over the world.[16]

Poverty had been around for a very long time. By the mid-1960s King was convinced that there was one major new factor: nations like the United States had the technology to completely eradicate poverty. The question was whether politicians and the wealthy had the will or moral resolve to do so. The continuation of poverty was compelling evidence that they did not.

Eliminate War and Internationalize Nonviolence

Martin Luther King understood that social problems are complex and interrelated phenomena. As such they affect and are affected by each other. Ultimately they all must be addressed because each adversely affects some segment of the population. War, particularly at a time when a number of countries possess highly sophisticated precision-guided missile systems and a substantial number of nuclear warheads, is an especially important issue to be addressed. Since a number of nations have the capability of literally destroying the entire world, concern about solving social problems such as racism and poverty will be moot if the world no longer exists. Consequently, no matter what other social problems are being addressed, it will be necessary to work toward eliminating militarism and war.

King finally broke silence regarding the war in Vietnam in 1967. Thereafter he could not speak and preach about war without also acknowledging the clear link to racism and poverty. He saw that there were twice as many blacks dying in Vietnam as whites in proportion to their percentage of the population. This, he believed, was a clear indication that blacks were victims of racism *and* economic

133

exploitation. Because of racism blacks were more vulnerable to poverty, substandard education, unemployment, and underemployment. Because there were few educational and employment opportunities, blacks enlisted in the armed forces in higher numbers. They did so not because it was their preferred choice, but because other choices were even less attractive. So they enlisted and reenlisted, and died in combat in disproportionately higher numbers than whites.[17]

Acknowledging that his earlier silence regarding the war was a betrayal of his moral conscience and his call to ministry, King announced that even before he was a civil rights leader and the recipient of countless awards, he had answered God's call to ministry. He was much more than a civil rights leader, he said. In 1965 he reacted to critics by saying, "I happen to be a minister of the Gospel. I'm the pastor of a church and in that role I have a priestly function as well as a prophetic function, and in the prophetic role I must constantly speak to the moral issues of our day far beyond civil rights."[18] The church, he declared, had been silent for too long on war in general and the Vietnam War in particular.

On April 4, 1967, precisely one year to the day before his assassination, King delivered what is arguably his most important address, "A Time to Break Silence," at the Riverside Church in New York City, in a meeting sponsored by Clergy and Laity Concerned. His decision to speak out had less to do with politics and everything to do with his sense of morality and what he believed to be right and wrong regarding the taking of human life. He had come home to principles that guided his ministry from the beginning: his convictions that Christianity is serious business and that the Christian's ultimate allegiance is to God only.[19] Christians are therefore called to do what is moral, not what is politically correct.

In that famous speech King enumerated six reasons he felt compelled to break silence and to liberate his moral conscience on Vietnam:

1. The war and the government's announced War on Poverty were connected. The escalating troop buildup meant massive dollars were being siphoned from the poverty program.
2. Exorbitant numbers of the poor were being sent to fight and die in the war. Black and white soldiers

135

were required to fight together in Vietnam but could not live in the same neighborhood or attend the same schools back home.

3. It was inconsistent to urge blacks in northern ghettos to be nonviolent, without having first given that same advice "to the greatest purveyor of violence in the world today—my own government."

4. Speaking against the war was consistent with the founding motto of the SCLC: "To save the soul

of America." King said further: "If America's soul becomes totally poisoned, part of the autopsy must read Vietnam."

5. The Nobel Peace Prize "was also a commission to work harder than [he] had ever worked"[20] in the quest for community.

6. King acknowledged a "vocation of sonship and brotherhood" that transcended race, nation, and creed. As God has a special concern for the oppressed and the voiceless, King understood that he had a responsibility to speak for them and to help them find their own voice.[21]

King appreciated President John F. Kennedy's saying that "mankind must put an end to war or war will put an end to mankind." If the universe hinges on a moral foundation, if life is truly worth living, if persons are truly sacred because they are imbued with God's image and loved by God, King concluded, then violence of all kinds—all over the world—must give way to *a consistent ethic of nonviolence*. This must be the case in a universe founded on morality. If the world house God has provided for us is to have any chance of surviving, nonviolence as a way of life must be internationalized.

Martin Luther King was enough of a realist to know that even though moral conscience demands such a stance, virtually no political leader or politician will agree to it in practice. Nevertheless, King rejected any notion of a sacred-secular dichotomy or moral dualism and insisted that religion—especially the Christian religion—is relevant in *every* area of life each and every day. He declared, "We must come to see that the god of religion is the god of life and that the god of Sunday is the god of Monday."[22] For people of goodwill who truly believe that human life is sacred, the internationalization of nonviolence as a creed or philosophy must be the ultimate *moral* ideal, regardless of what is done politically. Such people, King concluded, must "come with a massive act of conscience and say in the words of the old Negro spiritual, 'We ain't goin' study war no more.'"[23]

Because of King's fundamental Christian personalist stance about the interrelated structure of reality, it is theologically sound to say that any struggle for civil rights and against racism must also—at the very least—be a witness against poverty, economic exploitation, militarism, and war. King's theological social ethic makes it impossible for one to claim to be concerned about racism while inten-

tionally turning away from the devastating consequences of economic exploitation and the militaristic behavior of the United States and other nations. The Kingian ethic also has implications for other major concerns, some of which are discussed in the next chapter.

CHAPTER EIGHT

Women, Capital Punishment, and Homosexuality

Martin Luther King was interested in human rights and justice for all people. His Christian personalism and his theological social ethic required that he address any injustice of which he was aware. At the time of his assassination it is unknown whether King had clarity on the matter of women's rights. He was the victim of blindness caused by socialization in a patriarchal system. However, there is convincing evidence that had he lived into the early years of the 1970s he would have become a strong proponent of women's rights because he would have seen the injustice of the denial of their civil rights.

King was on record early regarding his opposition to capital punishment. And although there was no overt gay rights movement in his day, there is disagreement within the King family and among others as to whether he would be supportive of gay rights were he alive today. Bernice King, the youngest of King's children, has spoken and marched against gay rights. The two sons, Martin and Dexter, believe that everything about King's theology and practice unequivocally places him in the camp of supporting gay rights. This opinion was shared by King's late wife, Coretta, and late daughter, Yolanda.

The following provides a brief discussion on King's view of women, capital punishment, and homosexuality. Entire books can be—indeed should be—written on any one of these. In light of his theological social ethic, where would King likely stand on these matters were he alive today?

Women

Martin Luther King's commitment to an ethic of human dignity is in principle inclusive of all people, regardless of gender, race, age, sexuality, or class. The one place we easily detect inconsistency is in the area of gender distinctions in the public arena. In some ways King was as traditional in his thinking about women's public roles as most men before, during, and even since his day. But in some ways he exhibited quite progressive tendencies. Since King's is an ethic of human dignity, it is reasonable to think that there can be no place in his thought and practice that opens the door to male chauvinism on any level regarding women's roles. Nevertheless, we find that King himself came up short in this regard. How may we account for this inconsistency? This is not an easy question to answer, and to date it is one that has not been thoroughly examined. However, until this is done there are several things that can be said.

Sexism is gender stereotyping of men and women in a hierarchical sense, with men as superior to women. The term "sexism" had not been introduced before King's assassination in 1968. Robin Morgan was among the first to use the term in the introduction to her edited anthology *Sisterhood Is Powerful* (1970). The term that was in usage prior to this was "chauvinism," and by all accounts it applied to King and the black male leadership of the SCLC.

It might be argued that even though King would have favored the idea of women receiving equal rights, we are still left with trying to make sense of his chauvinistic behavior regarding women affiliated with the SCLC.

Consider the situation of Ella Baker. She was in many respects the best, most experienced organizer in the SCLC, yet her leadership was seldom formally acknowledged. All officers were men, mostly Baptist preachers. But it was Baker who set up the SCLC operation on a shoestring budget, with no staff support and no office space. She contributed significantly to organizing the Prayer Pilgrimage for Freedom held at the Lincoln Memorial on the third anniversary of the *Brown* decision in 1957. She was also the lead organizer of the SCLC's first independent campaign a few months later—the Crusade for Citizenship. The goal was to double the number of black voters in the South and to encourage them to be proactive in fighting for their rights. The more the male leaders ignored Baker's contributions, the more difficult it became. In fact, John Lewis has written of the "poisoned" relationship that developed between Ella Baker and the SCLC board, claiming that she was alienated early on, "not necessarily from Dr. King," but from other men in the organization.[1] Baker would have been an excellent SCLC officer. "But she was a woman," Lewis wrote, "a woman born at the wrong time."

Even when Baker, Septima Clark, Dorothy Cotton, and others were permitted to be in leadership positions in the SCLC, the traditional patriarchal values that dominated King's and the other males' practice frequently took over, making it difficult for them to acknowledge the constructive contributions of the women. Although Septima Clark was convinced, for instance, that King was appreciative and supportive of her work with citizenship education, she was just as convinced that, like other black ministers in the organization, he "didn't think too much of the way women could contribute." She cited the example that women were never allowed to put themselves on the meeting agenda.[2] Diane Nash Bevel, a leader in the early freedom rides, also reported on black males' trivialization of her contributions. Although King did not expressly participate in such behaviors with his male peers, neither did he intervene on behalf of the women.

Andrew Young, one of King's closest advisors and friends, said that King "was oblivious to the existence of any issues of his staff regarding gender equity. . . . He was not aware of his tendency to ignore [Septima Clark's] substantive comments or undervalue her work."[3] Most men of the era were oblivious to how they treated women as inferiors. Young put his finger on another important aspect of this complex issue when he wrote, "Ella Baker was a determined

woman and she reminded [King and the other Baptist ministers] of the strong Mommas they were all trying to break free of. The Baptist Church had no tradition of women in independent leadership roles, and the result was dissatisfaction all around [with Baker]."[4] Young confessed that most of the ministers—including himself, a Congregational minister—had grown up in households with strong, domineering mothers, and Baker reminded them of that. In a telling comment Young said:

> We had a hard time with domineering women in SCLC because Martin's mother, quiet as she was, was really a strong, domineering force in that family. She was never publicly saying anything but she ran Daddy King and she ran the church and she ran Martin, and so Martin's problems in the early days of the movement were directly related to his need to be free of that strong matriarchal influence.[5]

Although the situation was much more complex than Young makes it appear, unquestionably a strong, determined woman in public leadership (like Ella Baker) was more than a match for King.

We saw in chapter 2 that Coretta King conceded that her husband was the head of their family, but this did not mean for her that men are to seek to rule over women in the home. Remember, Coretta and Martin deleted the promise to "obey" from their wedding vows. King himself made the same point about male headship in a poignant way in a Mother's Day sermon in 1955:

> Men must accept the fact that the day has passed when the man can stand over the wife with an iron rod asserting his authority as "boss." This does not mean that women no longer respect masculinity

> [*sic*], i.e., strong, dynamic manliness. . . . But it does mean that the day has passed when women will be trampled over and treated as some slave subject to the dictates of a despotic husband.[6]

King applauded Christianity for helping to lift the status of women from that of mere childbearers to one of dignity, honor, and respect: "Women must be respected as human beings and not be treated as mere means. Strictly speaking, there is no boss in the home; it is no lord-servant relationship."[7] He clearly argued against headship, at least the traditional practice of men lording it over women in the home. In this regard King was quite progressive in his outlook regarding women.

Nevertheless, Coretta King was convinced that when it came to his own wife, "it was the female role he was most anxious for me to play," such as "being a homemaker and a mother for his children," and being home waiting for him at the end of the workday.[8] This was the tradition in which King, like most men, was socialized. Men, however, were to respect the woman's role and expected the woman to respect the man's.

Interestingly, King also exhibited a real sensitivity regarding women's roles. Coretta King was herself a highly educated, strong, self-determined woman. In addition, during his pastorate at Dexter and later as associate pastor at Ebenezer, King was virtually surrounded by educated, strong-willed, professional women and therefore knew firsthand of their abilities in leadership roles in the public sector. According to Coretta King, he even encouraged her "to teach or to give concerts if I wanted to so I could be independent."[9]

Perhaps the most that can be said on this point is that there was clear ambivalence in King's stance on women.

When a church woman wrote to his "Advice for Living" column in *Ebony* and inquired what she should do about a husband who was a pillar of the church but a tyrant at home, King gave three suggestions, one of which was very traditional, in which he raised the possibility that the woman was at fault. "I would suggest," he said, "that you analyze the whole situation and see if there is anything within your personality that arouses this tyrannical response from your husband."[10] It was the suggestion of a traditionalist, not different from that which King gave the woman who wrote to ask whether as a general rule she should adhere to her more conservative view about retaining her virginity until married. It surely was reasonable for a pastor to say that one "should hold firm to the principle of premarital virginity," as he advised. But a further statement was problematic: "Real men still respect purity and virginity within women."[11] Obviously, this implies a double standard for women and men. One can't help but wonder whether King also believed that "real" women respect and expect the same thing in men.

Regarding the feminist question, Stewart Burns is wrong when he says of King, "Given his background and his own patriarchal assumptions, he simply would not have understood where [radical feminists] were coming from."[12] In truth, the women's movement was peripheral for King in 1966 and 1967 since during much of that period he was overwhelmed with other major issues: his own desire to break silence over the war in Vietnam, and having to deal with issues of leadership, staffing, fundraising, the poverty question, the Poor People's Campaign, and so forth. These are not listed as "excuses" for King's blindness to the women's movement but as urgent issues with which he was preoccupied.

The National Organization for Women (NOW) formed in late 1966, less than two years before King was assassinated. However, King was a man of reason who was always open to new ideas, especially when buttressed by current events. Had leaders of the women's movement actually met with King, explained their agenda, and helped him remove his patriarchal blinders to see that theirs too was a civil rights or justice issue, they would very likely have received his unqualified endorsement and support.

Presently we can only speculate about how King would have received the formidable Pauli Murray—Afrikan American, member of the American Civil Liberties Union (ACLU) board, staunch defender of the sex discrimination provision of Title VII of the 1964 Civil Rights Act, and co-founder of NOW. At the very least he would have gone on record in support of women's rights. For no one was

149

quicker to acknowledge justice issues than Martin Luther King. Yet one wonders what King knew about the sex discrimination provision of Title VII and when. What did he know about President Kennedy's appointment of a national Commission on the Status of Women in 1961 and the comprehensive report it produced in 1963? What is known for certain is that King's ethic of dignity would have required his support of the women's movement had this been clearly within his moral field of awareness.

Capital Punishment

Criminologists have reported over many decades that racism and classism are at the heart of the practice of capital punishment in the United States. Any argument in favor of capital punishment in this country invariably produces a smoke screen to conceal race and class factors. In comparison to their percentage in the nation's overall population, an exorbitant number of black males continue to be on death row. In addition, large numbers of death row inmates are the poor of all races.

In chapter 6 we encountered the case of sixteen-year-old Jeremiah Reeves, who was accused of raping a white woman in Montgomery. Police officials forced Reeves to confess. When he was found guilty after a two-day trial and sentenced to death by electrocution (after the jury had deliberated for a mere thirty-four minutes) the case was appealed to the Supreme Court and a new trial was ordered. The result was the same, and Reeves was executed.

One can easily reason from King's ethic of dignity and his thoroughgoing ethic of nonviolence that he was against capital punishment. In his November 1957 "Advice for Living" column he responded to a person who inquired as to whether God approves the death penalty for crimes such as rape and murder. King wrote, "I do not think God approves the death penalty for any crime—rape and murder included."[13] God's concern is that people be improved and brought to conversion, a stance that is also consistent with the rehabilitation-reformation model of sentencing. The chief aim, King believed, must be the reformation of the criminal, not punishment. He therefore rejected the retribution or "just desserts" model of criminal sentencing.

What is most significant is that King's opening response to the person who inquired about the death penalty was that *God does not approve of it*, regardless of the alleged crime. What was really fundamental to him was *God's expectation*, which means that his primary response was a theological

one. King then appealed to the stance of the criminologist in support of his theological claim that "above all" capital punishment is "against the highest expression of love in the nature of God."[14] Although King did not say so expressly, he implied in this response that capital punishment is a sin against humanity and against God. Ultimately, capital punishment was a moral issue for King. "It is a question of the dignity of man," he said. Moreover, it did not matter to him that the method was electrocution (as in the case of Jeremiah Reeves) or poison gas.[15]

Homosexuality

Approximately two months after the Montgomery bus boycott began, Bayard Rustin arrived to advise and instruct King on the theory and practice of Gandhian nonviolence. Although there were periodic disagreements between them, King was a willing and eager student. Before too long, however, circumstances about Rustin made it necessary for him to leave Montgomery and to distance himself from King, although he continued to advise him long-distance.

Rustin was homosexual and had been arrested for a public homosexual act in California in 1953. When Rustin met King he was up-front about the matter, as well as having once been a member of the Communist Party. King gave no indication of being troubled by his sexuality. On reflection, Rustin said he did not know for certain how King felt about his sexuality, adding in 1987 that King "would have been sympathetic and would not have had the prejudicial view. Otherwise he would not have hired me."[16] Only when his orientation became a concern to the movement did it become an issue for King, said Rustin. When the talk and innuendoes began, King set up a committee to advise him. The group decided that both King and the movement would be harmed if Rustin remained. Rustin was convinced that King was never happy about his leaving Montgomery.

What is important is that upon first meeting Rustin and being told by him that he was homosexual, King, a black Baptist preacher—despite his political concern for the well-being of the boycott—displayed no immediate moral concern about this. It is also important that there is no indication that he secretly joked about Rustin's sexuality or that of one of his (King's) Baptist ministerial lieutenants

who was also homosexual.[17] Indicators are that King simply accepted Rustin as a human being who was committed to the cause of civil rights. At least one biographer on Rustin contends that King preferred that Rustin be a closeted homosexual.[18] Indeed, Rustin himself said that he was genuinely accepted in the movement "so long as I didn't declare that I was gay."[19]

At this writing I know of only one place where Martin Luther King made an explicit statement about homosexuality. In a January 1958 "Advice for Living" column a young man wrote to ask what he should do about feeling "about boys the way I ought to feel about girls." The young man himself clearly held a traditional view about the matter, and King gave a traditional response. "Your problem," King said, "is not at all an uncommon one." This was the old-line view. The homosexual has a *problem*, quite likely one that was "not an innate tendency, but something that has been culturally acquired." It was psychologically induced and repressed, which meant that he needed to seek professional psychiatric help in order to get "back to some of the experiences and circumstances that lead to the habit."[20] King ended by saying that the young man was on the right track inasmuch as he openly and honestly acknowledged that he had a "problem."

Interestingly, in his response to the young man King did not appeal to biblical texts, to which opponents of homosexuality generally appeal for supposedly definitive evidence that the Bible is against it and considers it sin. Of course, even had King cited scriptural texts he then would have needed to resort to what he himself characterized as the best in the liberal theology tradition: "its devotion to the search for truth, its insistence on an open and analytical mind, its refusal to abandon the best light of reason. Its contribution to the philological-historical criticism of biblical literature has been of immeasurable value."[21] King did not appeal to this in the present case. Furthermore, as noted previously, around age thirteen King was already publicly rejecting the idea of the inerrancy of the Bible. His experience at Morehouse College helped to liberate his thinking about the Bible. It was at Morehouse that "the shackles of fundamentalism" were loosed from him. "More and more," he wrote, "I could see a gap between what I had learned in Sunday school and what I was learning in college."[22] He was by no means a biblical literalist. However, it is also of interest that King did not cite contradictory evidence in psychiatry, an interesting omission since

he had such a strong appreciation for the contributions of the sciences in general, including social, behavioral, and medical science.

As a staunch personalist King's method was the analytic-synoptic method that requires the examination of all available relevant evidence. We learned previously that he was much influenced by Hegel's dictum that the true is the whole. Yet when asked for advice about homosexuality there is no evidence that he adhered to this principle. As a theologically trained clergyman the very least he should have done was provide the pros and cons of biblical contributions and shared his own theological reflection on the matter. He consistently did no less than this when addressing matters of race, class, and war.

Regarding homosexuality in the late 1950s, however, King seemed comfortable with that school of psychiatrists who argued that homosexuality is a mental disease. While this was not a unanimous position among psychiatrists of his day, it was the most commonly held view. King apparently was not aware of those who held a more middle line view, including Freud, whom he frequently quoted regarding other issues but whose work concerning homosexuality King apparently did not know. Freud and others rejected the idea that homosexuality as such was a sickness or disease. Others, of course, later challenged the assumption that homosexuality necessarily represents a psychiatric abnormality, claiming that it is no more abnormal than heterosexuality.

It is unclear whether King's views expanded in the ten years following the column's publication. In fairness it should be pointed out that it was not until 1974—six years after King was assassinated—that the Trustees of the American Psychiatric Association voted unanimously to remove homosexuality from the organization's official listing of mental disorders. Henceforth it would be seen as one form of sexual behavior, and not necessarily a deviant one.

When King wrote the column in 1958, he had only recently been appointed president of the newly formed SCLC. He was essentially consumed with trying to figure out how to continue the struggle for civil rights, which also included determining whether or not he should continue as senior pastor at Dexter Avenue Baptist Church. No wonder he gave a traditional response indicating he had not done more serious theological reflection on homosexuality.

What do we make of these considerations of King's ideas

on women, capital punishment, and homosexuality? We know that King, formally trained in systematic theology, was clearly more interested in *doing* theological social ethics than writing academic treatises on theology.[23] The die was cast—he would not be an academic theologian who spent his time engaging in theological and ethical reflection, teaching students, and writing systematic textbooks on theology. He continued to be interested in the world of academic theology and periodically talked about it in interviews, but he knew for him it was not to be.

But we have also seen that no matter where King's focus was in any particular civil rights campaign, he was always concerned about eradicating racism and always saw the connections between racism and whatever issue was being addressed at the time. We have also seen that current events, along with King's refinement of ideas and his

expanding experience—consistent with his personalist method—led to expansion of his moral outlook and his willingness to devote attention and energy to other social issues such as poverty and war. There is little doubt that expansion into other issues was probable had he lived longer.

CHAPTER NINE

The Legacy of
Martin Luther King Jr.

What is Martin Luther King's legacy for us today? King was a hardheaded realist who knew that in the affairs of human beings the political dimension must always be taken into consideration. However, his religious faith and commitment to the God of the Hebrew prophets and Jesus Christ was such that he chose to be *morally* correct, rather than *politically* correct. This must be the case, since he believed that God is the God of the whole world, seven days a week. Lewis V. Baldwin rightly places King in "that tradition which refuses to separate religious faith and moral considerations from politics, legal matters, and social reformism."[1]

The God of Sunday is also the God of Monday through Saturday. This conviction kept King at odds with the powers, including religious leaders and even at times leaders of other civil rights organizations. But what does such a conviction mean for us today?

Much of this chapter is a prophetic challenge to persons of all major religious faiths but particularly for Christians. Martin Luther King intentionally sought to apply the basic principles of his theology and faith to making the world a gentler, sweeter place for those living at the margins. As a man of ideas who, despite his own moral shortcomings, was faithful to God's call to the very end, he dreamed of and struggled to achieve a world in which human beings would actualize the beloved community. This is a commu-

nity in which all persons, regardless of race, gender, class, ability, age, nationality, and sexuality will be honored and treated with respect just because they are human beings created in God's image and loved by God.

Moreover, several aspects of King's theological social ethics make clear his sense of the inherent dignity not only of human beings but of nonhuman life-forms and the environment. There is no question that, like his personalist teachers as well as his father, maternal grandfather, and his teachers at Morehouse College, King focused more heavily on the dignity of human beings than of nonhuman life-forms. Yet he knew full well that it makes no sense to fight for human rights if one does not also fight for preserving and enhancing a world in which life is sustainable. That King did not focus as much on animal life and the environment does not mean he was not concerned about their well-being.

Action as Test of Belief

From the beginning of his ministerial vocation Martin Luther King lived by the conviction that reason and ideas are crucial to what we humans do in the world, but he advocated just as strongly that what matters most is not what one believes or how well one reasons things out. *What matters most is what one does.* It is admirable for someone to believe that every person possesses inherent dignity and sacredness because God is at the center of the universe guiding the destiny of life. But what was much more admirable and important for King was that one consistently live one's life in ways that actualize this principle.

It is not enough to teach, preach, lecture, and write about the inherent inviolable sacredness of persons if, in the presence of injustice and the dehumanization of persons one—for whatever reason—opts to do nothing. King was frequently critical of Christians and other people of goodwill who were afraid to take a public stand against injustice out of fear of standing alone. He sought to combine ideas and action, belief and deeds, theology and ethics. Not what we shout from pulpits and lecterns, or say we believe, but what we do is what matters in the end. Indeed, as early as 1954 Martin Luther King was using language that anticipated liberation theologies of the late 1960s. He said, "A man will do what he believes and in the final analysis he is what he does. There can be no divorce between belief and action. There might be some divorce between intellectual assent and action. Intellectual assent is merely agreeing that a thing is true; real belief is acting like it is true. Belief always takes a flight into action. The ultimate test for what a man believes is not what he says, but what he does."[2] This is a basic principle of liberation theology.

Too many religious people declare easily that they are Christian, Jewish, or Muslim. They assert that love and justice are at the heart of their faith, but they live in ways contrary to this. King's challenge is that such people must *think* about what it means to be members of a specific religious community, and then develop the courage and character to truly *live* their faith.

Need for Prophecy

In addition, the message of the Hebrew prophets of the eighth century BCE (Amos, Micah, and Isaiah) was central to King's theological social ethic. No Christian social activist of his day was as intoxicated with the spirit of justice for the least (i.e., the poor and marginalized) as Martin Luther King. He consistently advocated the need for a prophetic critique of life and thus the need for the church to be a "radical opposer of the status quo." The church that supports the status quo either by its silence or its actual support is not the church of Jesus Christ; it is not, King said, the hope of the world. King confronted this phenomenon from Montgomery to Memphis—this unwillingness of the church to stand up for justice and reject the status quo. "One of the basic responsibilities that Christianity has to society and to individuals is that of condemnation," King said. "The Church must forever stand in judgement upon every political, social and economic system, condemning evil wherever they exist."[3]

King believed that especially in times of social and political turmoil it is important for Christian ministers to *stress the need for prophecy.* "Not every minister can be a prophet, but some must be prepared for the ordeals of this high calling

and be willing to suffer courageously for righteousness."[4] Although technically correct in his claim that not every minister can be a prophet, everything we know about King's ministry and theology tells us that he believed that every minister, indeed every Christian, is duty bound to be prophetic in the face of injustice, since God expects justice to be done in the world. The church's great moral responsibility is to stand firm against the powers and demand—in the name of the One it represents—that justice be done. And here the emphasis is not on the mere generalization that justice be done. Rather, the church, as King understood it, must *name* the specific social evil or injustice and then declare in word and deed a vociferous *No* to it, and an equally loud *Yes* to God's requirement that justice be done. This means that the church should never find itself on the side of the powers and principalities.

Revolution of Values

There is a third general challenge that King's theological social ethic offers. His insistence on *the need for a revolution of values* is as important today as in his own time. In a way this goes to the heart of King's Christian personalism. This conception requires that society and the world use things and love people. King saw that when things "are considered more important than people, the giant triplets of racism, materialism and militarism are incapable of being conquered."[5] Everywhere King looked, including the church, he could see that in actuality what was held up as most important were impersonal objects or things and not persons. People, particularly those at the margins and others who have been historically excluded, continue (even now) to be treated as purely instrumental values, that is, as means to the ends of politicians, wealthy businesspeople, and oth-

ers. According to King's theological social ethics, every person is inherently valuable and thus is not to be used as an instrument for others' ends.

Martin Luther King reminded us that a true revolution of values means that the entire socioeconomic structure of this country needs to be radically transformed. A true revolution of values means that no one with even a modicum of moral sensitivity will be content in a society characterized by devastating poverty on the one hand, and extravagant wealth on the other. A true revolution of values is what is required in an internationalist or world house perspective. By being loyal to the entire human race, we may better be able to preserve and even enhance the best in our respective groups. In addition, King added the element of *urgency* to this need for a revolution of values. It needs to happen sooner rather than later.

We have seen that from the beginning to the end of his

ministry King openly criticized and fought against racism. He knew that racism was embedded in the very structures of this society, and while he was critical of the racism of individual whites, he fought hardest against institutional forms of it. Moreover, he sought to unmask the racism of those otherwise well-meaning whites who tried to conceal their hatred by attending church on Sunday morning, thinking that by not lynching or openly participating in the lynching of blacks it was a sign that they were not racists. King knew that every white person, no matter how liberal and well meaning, benefited from racism and unearned privileges. Although he was not into name calling, he was adamant that all white persons were responsible for how they responded to racism, whether they were individual racists or not.

To this point the emphasis has been on King's more general legacy to church and world. The remainder of this chapter focuses on his legacy to Afrikan Americans, for even though King exhibited the trait of internationalism long before the Montgomery campaign, he always under-stood that it is quite reasonable for individual groups to be concerned about their own well-being. Groups get into trouble when they seek such well-being and group loyalty at the expense of other groups. Otherwise King was quite at home with the idea of a healthy sense of group or national pride.

Assertion of Self-Worth

According to King, the very first thing blacks need to do is "to massively assert our dignity and worth."[6] This was an absolute imperative for a group that historically had been denied so much—denied even the human right of asserting their sense of humanity and dignity. When a group has

been subjected to such treatment as long as Afrikan Americans have, it is a massive challenge to reverse the sense that so many have that they are either not quite as good as white people, or that they are simply nobody. King's message was that blacks themselves must rise up and unequivocally affirm their sense of humanity and dignity.

Furthermore, black adults must begin instilling this sense of dignity in black children as soon as they are able to comprehend its meaning. What King said in his last SCLC presidential address is what he would say today were he alive, especially in light of the tragic phenomenon of black against black violence and murder among young Afrikan American males and the absolutely devastating sense of meaninglessness and lovelessness that pervades the lives of far too many of them. (I have altered some of King's language):

> Blacks will only be free when they reach down to the inner depths of their own being and sign with the pen and ink of assertive personhood their own emancipation proclamation. And, with a spirit straining toward true self-esteem, Blacks must boldly throw off the manacles of self-abnegation and say to themselves and to the world, "I am somebody. I am a person . . . with dignity and honor. I have a rich and noble history."[7]

Afrikan American boys who love themselves, their people, and are aware of the best in their cultural history do not commit senseless acts of violence and murder on each other and other members of their community.

The need to instill in black boys and black girls the sense of somebodyness that King stressed is crucial for the survival and health of the Afrikan American community. One who possesses a sense of somebodyness is not ashamed of his blackness and will do nothing to desecrate or destroy black life. In this regard King said, "Our children must be taught to stand tall with their heads proudly lifted. . . . This spirit, this drive, this rugged sense of somebodyness is the first and most vital step that [Blacks] must take."[8] To this, King maintained, should be added a related element, namely, a much healthier sense of group identity—pride and unity, not uniformity or exclusivity. If Afrikan Americans are to function at their best in all areas of life in this country, group identity, unity, pride, and trust will be necessary. Since this has been lacking for so long, it will take the indomitable will and relentlessness of individuals and the group to succeed.

Responsible for How We Respond

Martin Luther King also left a very tough word for his people around the issue of *self-determination and responsibility*. He was completely aware of and sensitive to the fact that systemic racism and economic exploitation are the root causes of much that has gone wrong in Afrikan American communities. As far back as 1958 he said, "The 'behavior deviants' within the Negro community stem from the economic deprivation, emotional frustration, and social isolation which are the inevitable concomitants of segregation."[9]

ANOTHER LEGACY...

King nevertheless insisted that although blacks are not guilty of the causes of so much that negatively affects them, they and they alone are *responsible for how they respond to what is being done to them.* He challenged blacks to be self-critical regarding this and related matters. "We must not let the fact that we are the victims of injustice lull us into abrogating responsibility for our own lives," he said.[10] King was critical of the high crime rate in black communities in the South and the North, and of the tendency of the black middle class to live and spend beyond their means, and to spend on nonessentials rather than donate money to worthy causes and institutions in the black community.

This is a very tough word to convey to historically oppressed people, even if that word comes from a member of the community of the stature of Martin Luther King. Essentially King was acknowledging that no matter what the hereditary or environmental conditions are, or no matter what is happening to them politically, economically, and socially, blacks are still morally autonomous beings capable of deciding how to respond to their circumstances—apathetically or proactively and creatively.

King urged that persons respond to their circumstances with strength and courage, for this rests solely on decision, on one's capacity and willingness to respond morally and appropriately or not. King would be the first to say that Afrikan Americans are not morally responsible for the historic enslavement and present-day discrimination that are the real causes behind the exorbitantly high rates of high school dropouts among many young black people and the excessively high homicide rate among young black males, nor are they responsible for the high unemployment and underemployment rates among them and the fact that they continue to be paid less than whites for doing the same jobs. But none of these devastatingly unjust things undermines the fact that as persons, blacks are morally autonomous beings. As such they are responsible for the positive and negative steps they take, and how they respond to what happens to them.

Preaching at Dexter Avenue Baptist Church in 1953, King said that members were responsible for what they decide, or how they respond to what was before them: "We are not responsible for the environment we are born in, neither are we responsible for our hereditary circumstances. But there is a third factor for which we are responsible namely, the personal response which we make to these circumstances."[11] King cited Jesus Christ as one

who was born in disadvantageous environmental and hereditary circumstances but "had within himself a power of personal response which was destined to transform his circumstances." He also named Marian Anderson and Roland Hayes, Afrikan Americans who grew up in poverty-stricken areas of the country and also had to battle racial discrimination but still had the strength of courage and determination to respond to their environmental circumstances in ways that led to their names being etched into the history books. During the 1966 Christmas season King applauded and gave thanks for young black males of Chicago like Teddy, "a child of the slums . . . [who] decided to rise above the cruelties of those slums to work and march, peacefully, for human dignity."[12] The environment of these boys offered them little more than death-inducing alternatives, but they responded by joining the protest demonstrations.

No matter what the environmental and hereditary restrictions, King declared, blacks have within them *the capacity to respond* in life-enhancing rather than death-inducing ways. Reflecting on his experience with black boys in a Chicago slum, King said, "All their lives . . . [they] have known life as a madhouse of violence and degradation. Some have never experienced a meaningful family life."[13] To many of these impoverished inner-city boys this society has so limited the alternatives of their lives that they believe the only way to express their "manhood" is through violence.

But even so, King would remind us today that Afrikan American ancestors under the most vicious form of forced enslavement and dehumanization in the annals of history chose life rather than death. In addition, we have seen that black children and youth from Montgomery to Memphis chose life over death during the civil and human rights movements. They fought for the right to be human beings and all of those other constructive things that contribute to community making. King even spoke in high praise of inner-city gang members in Chicago who volunteered to join the Freedom March through Mississippi in 1966. In the face of unearned suffering of all kinds, earlier generations of Afrikan Americans chose life.

Martin Luther King was always challenging his people to accept responsibility for the things they can control. He made just such an appeal to a large crowd near the Alabama state capitol. The group had gathered in protest of the historic unjust treatment of blacks in the courts, and of the execution of young Jeremiah Reeves. Midway through his speech King challenged the mostly black crowd to accept their responsibility to do all in their power to improve themselves and their community. "Let us work at every hour for cleanliness, good manners, chastity, home improvement and neighborhood improvement," he said. "If we have shortcomings, let us face up to them honestly."[14] King was sensitive to the fact that many of the people he was addressing were dirt poor and could not find meaningful and gainful employment from which they could earn a living wage. But he also knew that after so many years of forced degradation, the process of reversing the sense of not being important or of being nobody had to begin somewhere. And what better place to begin than at the point where the crowd could decide anew how they would respond to the inhumane conditions forced on them? That one is forced to live in a rundown neighborhood does not mean that it is all right to throw trash on the street or to permit one's guests to do so. It is necessary to develop a positive attitude toward self and neighborhood, such that one does what one can to keep it clean and to be a good neighbor.

King's message to Afrikan Americans is simple: *We are responsible for the way we respond to the evils and injustices done to us.* Blacks and whites alike are responsible to and for those boys who pull the triggers of the guns that kill so many young blacks. Blacks and whites are also responsible for how they respond to the gun lobbyists, manufacturers, retailers, and policymakers.

My hope is that these armchair reflections on Martin Luther King will inspire readers to delve much more deeply into the study of King, particularly his sermons, speeches, and interviews. King was truly a man of ideas who was committed to social activism as a way to create openings for the emergence of the beloved community. Moreover, if we are to learn anything from this book, let it be to live our faith more boldly in every area of life, for no area of human existence is exempt from the relentless care and compassion of the God of the Hebrew prophets and Jesus Christ.

Notes

Preface

1. Throughout I use the term "white(s)" because it is the long-time custom. Commenting on the manuscript of the book, Professor Cheryl Kirk-Duggan suggested the use of "Euro-American," inasmuch as "no one is born white, they become white through socialization, privilege, and cultural expectations." She is here influenced by the work of Thandeka, *Learning to Be White* (New York: Continuum, 1999). Although Kirk-Duggan's suggestion comes too late to be inserted throughout this book, it will be manifested in subsequent writings by this author.
2. During the Black Consciousness Movement of the late 1960s a number of proponents adopted the use of "k" in the spelling of "Afrika," which was also consistent with the usage of many groups on the Afrikan continent as well. This is still the case today. For example the preferred spelling in a publication I receive from Accra, Ghana, *The Afrikan Crusader*, is "Afrikan" throughout. I adopted this spelling for my own writing after the publication of my first book in 1994.

1. Our Racist History

1. Andrew Hacker, *Two Nations: Black and White, Separate, Hostile, Unequal*, expanded and updated ed. (New York: Ballantine Books, 1995), 65.
2. Joe R. Feagin, *Systemic Racism* (New York: Routledge, 2006), 7.
3. Ibid., 8.
4. Joe R. Feagin, *Racist America* (New York: Routledge, 2000), 175.

5. Kevin Shillington, *History of Africa*, rev. ed. (New York: St. Martin's Press, 1989, 1995), 176.
6. Martin Luther King Jr., "The Meaning of Hope," December 10, 1967, King Library and Archives, 13.
7. Leslie Fishel Jr. and Benjamin Quarles, eds., "The Sentence of John Punch," in *The Negro American: A Documentary History* (New York: William Morrow & Co., 1967), 19.
8. Thomas Jefferson, "Notes on the State of Virginia," in *Thomas Jefferson: Writings*, ed. Merrill D. Peterson (New York: Literary Classics of the United States, 1984), 264, 265–66. The quote is from Query XIV.
9. Martin Luther King Jr., *Where Do We Go from Here: Chaos or Community?* (Boston: Beacon Press, 1967), 74–75.
10. Jefferson, "Notes on the State of Virginia," 266.
11. *Where Do We Go from Here,* 76.
12. Ibid., 77.
13. Even though they were not granted full constitutional rights, white women were included among "free persons."
14. "Meaning of Hope," 14. Here and elsewhere, citations to works by King will appear with title only after their first full citation.
15. Rayford Logan, *The Betrayal of the Negro* (New York: Collier Books, 1965), 23.
16. In one of many "atonement trials," the Justice Department reopened the Till murder case on May 10, 2004. A documentary by filmmaker Keith Beauchamp revealed new evidence that pointed to new witnesses who claimed that others, besides the now deceased (never convicted, self-confessed) murderers of Till, may have been involved and are still living.

2. Ideas from Home

1. Stephen B. Oates, *Let the Trumpet Sound* (New York: Harper & Row, 1982), 4.
2. Lerone Bennett Jr., *What Manner of Man: A Biography of Martin Luther King Jr.* (Chicago: Johnson Publishing Company, 1976), 18.

3. Martin Luther King Sr., *Daddy King: An Autobiography,* with Clayton Riley (New York: William Morrow & Co., 1980), 25.

4. *Papers*, 1:10. *Papers* refers herein to *The Papers of Martin Luther King Jr.*, ed. Clayborne Carson, 6 of 14 vols. published (Berkeley, CA: University of California Press, 1992–2007).

5. I have seen the term "social gospelism" in the literature, but no precise definition exists. For our purpose, it has to do with how one actually does social Christianity, i.e., how one applies Christian principles to solving social problems.

6. *Papers*, 1:10.

7. Lewis V. Baldwin, "Understanding Martin Luther King Jr. within the Context of Southern Black Religious History," *Journal of Religious Studies* 13, no. 2, (Fall 1987): 6.

8. Martin Luther King Jr., *Stride toward Freedom* (New York: Harper & Row, 1958), 90.

9. Garth Baker-Fletcher, *Somebodyness* (Minneapolis: Augsburg Fortress, 1993), 21–24.

10. Clayborne Carson, ed., *The Autobiography of Martin Luther King Jr.* (New York: Warner Books, 1998), 9.

11. Ibid.

12. Coretta Scott King, *My Life with Martin Luther King Jr.* (New York: Holt, Rinehart & Winston, 1969), 91.

3. Ideas from the Academy

1. *Autobiography*, 15.

2. Oates, *Let the Trumpet Sound*, 20.

3. See Martin Luther King Jr., *Stride toward Freedom*, 90–107, and his *Strength to Love* (New York: Harper & Row, 1963), 135–42.

4. *Stride toward Freedom*, 91.

5. Benjamin E. Mays, *Seeking to Be Christian in Race Relations,* rev. ed. (New York: Friendship Press, 1952), 8.

6. Quoted in Taylor Branch, *Parting the Waters* (New York: Simon & Schuster, 1988), 68.

7. *Papers*, 4:398.

8. G. W. F. Hegel, *The Phenomenology of Mind,* trans. J. B. Baillie (London: George Allen & Unwin, 1931), 81.

9. *Papers,* 3:281.

10. Hegel, *Phenomenology of Mind,* 233.

11. *Papers,* 3:454.

12. Ibid., 6:72.

13. *Stride toward Freedom,* 91.

14. *Papers,* 1:274.

15. The discussion in this and the next paragraph is heavily influenced by Michael G. Long's incisive book, *Against Us, But for Us: Martin Luther King Jr. and the State* (Macon, GA: Mercer University Press, 2002).

16. Bernard Ramm, *A Handbook of Contemporary Theology* (Grand Rapids: Wm. B. Eerdmans, 1966), 89.

17. *Autobiography,* 25.

18. Ibid., 31.

19. *Papers,* 6:387.

20. Ibid., 6:336.

21. See Rufus Burrow Jr., *Personalism: A Critical Introduction* (St. Louis: Chalice Press, 1999), and Burrow, *God and Human Dignity: The Personalism, Theology, and Ethics of Martin Luther King Jr.* (Notre Dame, IN: University of Notre Dame Press, 2006).

22. Martin Luther King Jr., "The Ethical Demands of Integration," in *A Testament of Hope,* ed. James M. Washington (New York: Harper & Row, 1986), 119.

23. *Papers,* 6:410.

4. Montgomery

1. *Autobiography,* 105, 197; *Stride toward Freedom,* 44.

2. Charles Emerson Boddie, *God's "Bad Boys"* (Valley Forge, PA: Judson Press, 1972), 70.

3. The Montgomery Improvement Association (MIA) was the organization established to provide leadership for the bus boycott. King was voted president.

4. Quoted in Stewart Burns, *To the Mountaintop* (San Francisco: HarperSanFrancisco, 2004), 105.
5. Ibid., 105.
6. Quoted in Lynne Olson, *Freedom's Daughters* (New York: Touchstone, 2001), 114.
7. Quoted in Burns, *To the Mountaintop*, 148.
8. Quoted in Olson, *Freedom's Daughters*, 122.
9. *Autobiography*, 208.
10. Quoted in Burns, *To the Mountaintop*, 117.

5. Christian Love and Gandhian Nonviolence

1. Bayard Rustin, *Reminiscences* (New York: Oral History Research Office, Columbia University, 1988), 140.
2. Ibid., 136.
3. *Papers*, 6:347.
4. *Stride toward Freedom*, 87.
5. *Strength to Love*, 105.
6. Nygren's claim that God is agape (in his book *Agape and Eros*, trans. Philip S. Watson [Philadelphia: Westminster Press, 1953], 210) is problematic to the degree that he fails to acknowledge that while it is the principle term for love in the Second Testament, there are a number of places in which *philia* is also used. This means that God may also be characterized as *philia*, especially since scholars have not been able to detect precise distinctions between the two terms (Karl Paul Donfried, "Love," in *The HarperCollins Bible Dictionary*, ed. Paul J. Achtemeier [San Francisco: HarperSanFrancisco, 1996], 625).
7. "My Trip to the Land of Gandhi," in *Testament of Hope*, 26.
8. *Papers*, 6:252.
9. *Papers*, 6:291.
10. *Strength to Love*, 133.
11. "Facing the Challenge of a New Age," in *Testament of Hope*, 141. [See also *Strength to Love*, 133.]
12. *Papers*, 6:200.

13. Ibid., 6:386.
14. Ibid., 6:382.
15. Ibid., 6:99.
16. "An Experiment in Love," in *Testament of Hope*, 17.
17. Ibid.
18. Martin Luther King Jr., "Letter from Birmingham Jail," in *Why We Can't Wait* (New York: Harper & Row, 1963), 81.
19. Ibid., 169.
20. Krishna Kripalani, ed., *All Men Are Brothers: Life and Thoughts of Mahatma Gandhi* (New York: Columbia University Press, 1969), 80.
21. "An Experiment in Love," in *Testament of Hope*, 19.
22. Ibid.
23. Quoted in Stewart Burns, *Daybreak of Freedom* (Chapel Hill: The University of North Carolina Press, 1997), 293.

6. The Power and Persuasion of Youth

1. *Papers*, 6:212.
2. Two excellent books inform the discussion in the remainder of this chapter: Ellen Levine, *Freedom's Children* (New York: G. P. Putnam's Sons, 1993), and David Halberstam, *The Children* (New York: Random House, 1998).
3. Levine, *Freedom's Children, 21.*
4. Ibid., 20.
5. Ibid.
6. Ibid., 27.
7. Ibid., 29.
8. *Why We Can't Wait*, 65.
9. Ibid., 79.
10. Ibid., 101.
11. Halberstam, *Children*, 438.
12. *Why We Can't Wait*, 102.
13. Ibid.
14. Diane McWhorter, *Carry Me Home: Birmingham, Alabama—The Climactic Battle of the Civil Rights Revolution* (New York: Touchstone Books, 2002), 386.
15. Ibid., 390.

16. Halberstam, *Children*, 441.
17. Ibid.
18. "Eulogy for the Martyred Children," in *Testament of Hope*, 221.
19. *Autobiography*, 230.
20. Halberstam, *Children*, 406.
21. Quoted in Levine, *Freedom's Children*, 113.
22. Halberstam, *Children*, 338.
23. *Autobiography*, 249.
24. Ibid., 250.
25. Ibid., 272.
26. Ibid., 275.
27. Ibid., 276.

7. Against Racism, Economic Exploitation, and War

1. "Transcript of 'Meet the Press' Television News Interview," in *Testament of Hope*, 408.
2. "Remaining Awake through a Great Revolution," in *Testament of Hope*, 270.
3. Ibid., 271.
4. Ibid., 270.
5. *Papers*, 6:112.
6. *Where Do We Go from Here*, 167.
7. Ibid., 190.
8. Martin Luther King Jr, "Remaining Awake though a Great Revolution," in *A Knock at Midnight*, ed. Clayborne Carson and Peter Holloran (New York: Warner Books, 1998), 207.
9. *Papers*, 6:105.
10. Ibid., 6:105, 326.
11. Ibid., 6:274.
12. *Where Do We Go from Here*, 173.
13. "Showdown for Nonviolence," in *Testament of Hope*, 64.
14. *Papers*, 6:220.
15. *Where Do We Go from Here*, 177.
16. "Remaining Awake though a Great Revolution," in *Testament of Hope*, 272.
17. "A Testament of Hope," in *Testament of Hope*, 326; "Tran-

script of 'Face to Face' Television News Interview," in ibid., 407.

18. From transcript of the Channel 2, KNXT-TV, Los Angeles program *Newsmakers*, July 10, 1965, King Library and Archives, 2.

19. *Papers*, 6:169, 341.

20. "A Time to Break Silence," in *Testament of Hope*, 234.

21. See ibid., 232–34.

22. *Papers*, 6:172.

23. "Remaining Awake though a Great Revolution" in *Testament of Hope*, 277.

8. Women, Capital Punishment, and Homosexuality

1. John Lewis (with Michael D'Orso), *Walking with the Wind* (New York: Simon & Schuster, 1998), 212.

2. Rosetta Ross, *Witnessing and Testifying* (Minneapolis: Fortress Press, 2003), 85.

3. Andrew Young, *An Easy Burden* (New York: HarperCollins, 1996), 139.

4. Ibid., 137.

5. Quoted in Nick Kotz and Mary Lynn Kotz, *A Passion for Equality: George A. Wiley and the Movement* (New York: W. W. Norton & Co., 1977), 252n.

6. *Papers*, 6:212.

7. Ibid., 6:212.

8. Coretta Scott King, *My Life with Martin Luther King Jr.*, 60.

9. Ibid., 91.

10. *Papers*, 4:305.

11. Ibid., 4:306.

12. Burns, *To the Mountaintop*, 374.

13. *Papers*, 4:305.

14. Ibid., 4:305.

15. *Why We Can't Wait*, 119–20.

16. Bayard Rustin, "Martin Luther King's View on Gay People," in Devon W. Carbado and Donald Weise, ed., *Time on Two Crosses: The Collected Writings of Bayard Rustin* (San Francisco: Cleis Press, 2003), 292.

17. John D'Emilio, *Lost Prophet* (New York: Free Press, 2003), 298.
18. Ibid., 372.
19. Rustin, "Black and Gay in the Civil Rights Movement," in *Time on Two Crosses*, 284.
20. *Papers*, 4:348.
21. *Autobiography*, 25.
22. Ibid., 15.
23. *Strength to Love*, 137.

9. The Legacy of Martin Luther King Jr.

1. Lewis V. Baldwin, introduction to *The Legacy of Martin Luther King Jr.* by Lewis V. Baldwin with Rufus Burrow Jr., Barbara Holmes, and Susan Holmes Winfield (Notre Dame, IN: University of Notre Dame Press, 2002), xv.
2. *Papers*, 6:171.
3. Ibid., 6:199.
4. *Stride toward Freedom*, 210.
5. *Where Do We Go from Here*, 186.
6. "Where Do We Go from Here?" in *Testament of Hope*, 245–46.
7. Ibid., 246.
8. *Where Do We Go from Here*, 123.
9. *Stride toward Freedom*, 222–23.
10. Ibid., 223.
11. *Papers*, 6:142.
12. "A Gift of Love," in *Testament of Hope*, 63.
13. Ibid., 62.
14. *Papers*, 4:398.

Select Bibliography

Books

Baldwin, Lewis V. *There Is a Balm in Gilead: The Cultural Roots of Martin Luther King Jr.* Minneapolis: Augsburg Fortress, 1991.

―――. *To Make the Wounded Whole: The Cultural Legacy of Martin Luther King Jr.* Minneapolis: Augsburg Fortress, 1992.

Branch, Taylor. *At Canaan's Edge: America in the King Years, 1965–68.* New York: Simon & Schuster, 2006.

―――. *Parting the Waters: America in the King Years, 1954–63.* New York: Simon & Schuster, 1988.

―――. *Pillar of Fire: America in the King Years 1963–65.* New York: Simon & Schuster, 1998.

Burns, Stewart. *To the Mountaintop.* San Francisco: HarperSanFrancisco, 2004.

Burrow, Rufus Jr. *God and Human Dignity: The Personalism, Theology, and Ethics of Martin Luther King Jr.* Notre Dame, IN: University of Notre Dame Press, 2006.

Carson, Clayborne, ed. *The Autobiography of Martin Luther King Jr.* New York: Warner Books, 1998.

―――, general ed. *The Papers of Martin Luther King Jr.* 6 of 14 vol. published. Berkeley, CA: University of California Press, 1992, 1994, 1997, 2000, 2005, 2007.

Oates, Stephen B. *Let the Trumpet Sound: The Life of Martin Luther King Jr.* New York: Harper & Row, 1982.

Washington, James M., ed. *A Testament of Hope: The Essential Writings of Martin Luther King Jr.* New York: Harper & Row, 1986.

Select Bibliography

DVDs

Citizen King. Eds. Ed Barteski and Jean-Philippe Boucicaut and produced, directed, written by Orlando Bagwell and W. Noland Walker (2004 WGBH Educational Foundation and ROJA Productions, Inc., 2004).

Eyes on the Prize: America's Civil Rights Movement. 7 vols., Henry Hampton, creator and executive producer, 1986, 1990; distributed by Public Broadcasting Service.

    Volume 1, *Awakenings (1954–1956)* and *Fighting Back (1957–1962)*, ed. Daniel Eisenberg and produced and directed by Judith Vecchione.

    Volume 2, *Ain't Scared of Your Jails (1960–1961)* and *No Easy Walk (1961–1963)*, ed. Charles Scott and produced, directed, written by James A. Devinney and Callie Crossley.

    Volume 3, *Mississippi: Is This America: (1962–1964)* and *Bridge to Freedom (1965)*, ed. Charles Scott and produced, directed, written by Callie Crossley and James A. Devinney.

    Volume 4, *The Time Has Come (1964–1966)* and *Two Societies (1965–1968)*, ed. Betty Ciccarelli and produced, directed, written by Sheila Bernard and Sam Pollard.

    Volume 5, *Power! (1966–1968)* and *The Promised Land (1967–1968)*, ed. Lillian Benson and produced, directed, written by Paul Stekkler and Jacqueline Shearer.

    Volume 6, *Ain't Gonna Shuffle No More (1964–1972)* and *A Nation of Law? (1968–1971)*, ed. Thomas Ott and produced, directed, written by Terry Kay Rockefeller, Thomas Ott and Louis Massiah.

    Volume 7, *The Keys to the Kingdom (1974–1980)* and *Back to the Movement (1979–1985)*, ed. Charles Scott and produced, directed, written by James A. Devinney and Madison Davis Lacy Jr.

Index

Abernathy, Ralph, 74, 77
"Advice for Living" column, 148, 154–55
agape, 87–89
ahimsa, 91–93
Alabama Christian Movement for Human Rights (ACMHR), 106
Alabama State College, 64, 69
Albany movement, 105
analytic-synoptic method, 156
Anderson, Marian, 174

Baker, Ella, 144, 145, 146
Baldwin, Lewis V., 38, 161–62
beloved community, 128, 162–63, 177
Bevel, Diane Nash, 108, 118, 145
Bevel, James, 107–8, 109, 113, 118
Birmingham, Alabama, 105–11
black social gospelism, 33

black women of Montgomery, 62, 64, 73, 74
"Bloody Sunday," 120
"Bombingham," 105
Borders, William Holmes, 33
Boston University, 45
Bradley, Mamie, 20
Braun, Carol Moseley, 15
Brooke, Edward, 15
Browder, Aurelia, 76
Browder v. Gayle, 72, 76
Brown Chapel AME Church, 119
Brown II, 19
Brown v. Board of Education, 19, 71
Bruce, Blanche K., 14
Burks, Mary Fair, 68, 69, 72
Burns, Stewart, 149

capital punishment, 150–52
Chaney, James, 114
children's crusade for freedom, 108
Chivers, Walter, 44, 54

Christian realism, 56
Civil Rights Act of 1964, 115
civil rights amendments, 14
Clark, Jim, 117, 118
Clark, Septima, 144–45
Collins, Addie Mae, 111
Colvin, Claudette, 71, 72–73, 76, 77, 99, 101
Commission on the Status of Women, 150
Connor, Eugene ("Bull"), 105, 106, 109, 111, 117
Constitution of United States, 10–12
Cotton, Dorothy, 144
Council of Federated Organizations (COFO), 114
Crozer Theological Seminary, 44

Daniel, Lucretia (Williams), 31
Deberry, Roy, 112

Index

Declaration of Independence, 10–12
Dexter Avenue Baptist Church, 62, 64, 66, 99, 104
dialectical process, 49–50
disinterested love, 88
DuBois, W. E. B., 32
"Dynamite Hill," 105

Easter, 48
Ebenezer Baptist Church, 24, 31, 104
Emancipation Proclamation, 14
Emerson, John, 12
ethical Christianity, 21

Feagin, Joe, 3–4
Fellowship of Reconciliation (FOR), 80
Founding Fathers, 10
"Freedom Summer," 114, 115–16

Gandhi, Mohandas K., 46, 82–83, 91, 92, 93
Gaston, A. G., 119
Gayle, W. A., 71, 76
Georgia Equal Rights League, 33
Good Friday, 48
Goodman, Andrew, 114
Gray, Fred, 76
Great Compromise (1877), 16

Greensboro Agricultural and Technical College, 104

Hacker, Andrew, 2–3
Halberstam, David, 109, 111
Hamer, Fannie Lou, 114
Harlan, John Marshall, 17
Hayes, Roland, 174
Hayes, Rutherford B., 116
Hegel, 49–50
homespun personalism, 37
homespun realism, 53
homosexuality, 153–58

internationalization of nonviolence, 137–38

Jefferson, Thomas, 9–10
Johns, Vernon, 65–68, 73

Kant, Immanuel, 58
Kelsey, George, 33, 43–44, 51, 54
King, Alfred Daniel (A. D.), 23
King, Bernice, 142
King, Coretta Scott, 40–41, 142, 146, 147
King, Delia, 28, 29–30
King, Dexter, 142

King, James Albert, 27–28
King, Martin Luther III, 142
King, Mike ("Daddy"), 28, 29, 30, 34–37, 39, 41
King, Willie Christine (Faris), 23
King, Yolanda, 142
Ku Klux Klan, 15–16, 17, 19, 112

Lacey, Joseph, 101–2
Lafayette, Bernard, 113, 116–17, 118
Lawson, James, 112
"Letter from Birmingham Jail," 91, 107
Lewis, John, 113, 118, 144
liberal theology, 54, 55
liberation theology, 164
Lincoln, Abraham, 14

Marshall, Thurgood, 119
Mays, Benjamin E., 33, 43, 44
McDonald, Susie, 76
McNair, Denise, 111
Mississippi Delta, 112–16
Montgomery, Alabama, ch. 4, 99, 101–5

Montgomery Improvement Association (MIA), 70, 105
Moore, Gladys, 72
moral law, 87
Morehouse College, 44, 45, 46
Moses, Bob, 118
Murray, Pauli, 149
Muste, A. J., 82

NAACP, 19, 33, 36, 68, 99, 101
National Organization for Women (NOW), 149
neo-orthodox theology, 54, 55
Niebuhr, Reinhold, 52, 53–56, 89, 90
Nixon, Edwin D. (E. D.), 68, 71–72, 74, 77
nonhuman life-forms, 163
nonviolence, 83–93
Nygren, Anders, 87, 88

Obama, Barak, 15
objective moral order, 46–48, 86–87

Parker, John Andrew, 31
Parker, Theodore, 48
Parks, Jennie Celeste (Williams), 32
Parks, Rosa, 21, 62–64, 68, 73, 77
Parks, William, 32

Pettus Bridge, 120
philosophy of personalism, 45, 57–59, 126, 127–28
Pilgrimage to Nonviolence, 46
Plessy, Homer, 17
poverty, 131–33
prophecy, 164–66
Punch, John, 8

racism, 129–31
Ramsey, Paul, 88
Rauschenbusch, Walter, 46, 52
Reconstruction, 14–15
Reese, Jeannetta, 76
Reeves, Jeremiah, 101, 103, 151, 152, 175
religious faith, 85–86
responsibility, 171
Revels, Hiram, 14
revolution of values, 166–68
Roberson, Bernita, 106–7
Robertson, Carole, 111
Robinson, JoAnn, 68, 69, 70, 72, 73
Rustin, Bayard, 80–82, 153–54

satyagraha, 90–91
Schwerner, Michael, 114
Scott, Dred, 12–13
Scott, Harriet, 12–13

self-worth, 168–70
Selma, Alabama, 116–18
"separate but equal," 17
Sermon on the Mount, 80
Shuttlesworth, Fred, 105–6
Shuttlesworth, Fred Jr., 106
Shuttlesworth, Pat, 106
Shuttlesworth, Ricky, 106
Simmons, William J., 17
sin, 56, 89–90, 129–30, 131
sit-in, 104–5
Sixteenth Street Baptist Church, 111
"slavery question," 5–10
Smiley, Glenn, 77
Smith, Mary Louise, 72, 76
SNCC, 112, 114, 118
Social and Political Action Committee, 70, 99
social gospel, 32, 33, 51–52
Southern Christian Leadership Conference (SCLC), 103
spirit of protest, 30

Taney, Roger B., 12, 13
Taylor, Fred, 103

Index

Till, Emmett, 19–20, 21

Title VII, 149, 150

training in nonviolence, 94–95

Tseung Qui Cho, 88

Vietnam, 124, 133–37

Vivian, C. T., 113

war, 133–36

Washington, Booker T., 32

Webb, Sheyann, 119–20

Wesley, Cynthia, 111

White Citizens Councils, 112

white privilege, 3

Williams, Adam Daniel (A. D.), 31–33, 35

Williams, Alberta Christine (King), 32, 35, 37–38

Williams, Hosea, 120

Williams, Jennie Celeste (Parks), 32, 33

Williams, Samuel, 33, 44, 51, 54

Williams, Willis, 31

women, 142–50

Women's Political Council (WPC), 69–71

world house perspective, 126–29

X, Malcolm, 119

Young, Andrew, 145–46

youth, Ch. 6

Zeitgeist, 64

CPSIA information can be obtained
at www.ICGtesting.com
Printed in the USA
FFOW03n1212190617
36902FF